Geography

D0243459

Also available in Oxford Minireference

Biology
Chemistry
Computing
Mathematics
Physics
Science
Twentieth-Century History

Minidictionary of
Geography

SUSAN MAYHEW

OXFORD UNIVERSITY PRESS
1994

Oxford University Press, Walton Street, Oxford OX2 6DP

Oxford New York Toronto
Delhi Bombay Calcutta Madras Karachi
Kuala Lumpur Singapore Hong Kong Tokyo
Nairobi Dar es Salaam Cape Town
Melbourne Auckland Madrid

and associated companies in
Berlin Ibadan

Oxford is a trade mark of Oxford University Press

© Oxford University Press 1994

All rights reserved. No part of this publication may be reproduced,
stored in a retrieval system, or transmitted, in any form or by any means,
without the prior permission in writing of Oxford University Press.
Within the UK, exceptions are allowed in respect of any fair dealing for the
purpose of research or private study, or criticism or review, as permitted
under the Copyright, Designs and Patents Act, 1988, or in the case of
reprographic reproduction in accordance with the terms of the licences
issued by the Copyright Licensing Agency. Enquiries concerning
reproduction outside these terms and in other countries should be
sent to the Rights Department, Oxford University Press,
at the address above

This book is sold subject to the condition that it shall not, by way
of trade or otherwise, be lent, re-sold, hired out or otherwise circulated
without the publisher's prior consent in any form of binding or cover
other than that in which it is published and without a similar condition
including this condition being imposed on the subsequent purchaser

British Library Cataloguing in Publication Data

Data available

Library of Congress Cataloging in Publication Data
Mayhew, Susan.
Minidictionary of geography / Susan Mayhew.
p.   cm.—(Oxford minireference)
1. Geography—Dictionaries.   I. Title.   II. Series.
910'.3—dc20   G63.M394   1994   93–46664

ISBN 0-19-211692-4 (pbk.)

10 9 8 7 6 5 4 3 2 1

Typeset by Oxuniprint
Printed in Great Britain by
Charles Letts (Scotland) Ltd.
Dalkeith, Scotland

How to use this book

Headwords are printed in bold type and appear in alphabetical order. However, some entries contain further definitions. These have been included under the headword to avoid unnecessary repetition and to show some of the wider applications of the headword.

Symbols

* before a word indicates a cross-reference to a separate entry for that term. In a few cases the cross-reference as indicated does not have the same wording as in the entry, but is close enough to make further reference possible.

▷ points out other related entries.

▷▷ refers the reader to the illustration for another entry.

✍ shows that an entry is itself illustrated. Sometimes it may be necessary to turn a page to find the illustration.

A

abiotic Not living; without life. This word is usually used to describe parts of *ecosystems.

abrasion The filing away of the surface as pieces of rock held in river or sea water, *glacier ice, or wind are pounded against it. Among other effects, abrasion can cut scratches on rocks in *glaciated regions, hollow out furrows in desert rocks, or cut a rocky stretch, known as an **abrasion platform**, at the foot of a cliff. ▷▷ marine erosion.

accessibility The ease or difficulty with which you can get to a location. An **accessible** place is easy to reach, and accessibility can be calculated by using a framework known as an **accessibility matrix**. To illustrate this, five towns are shown overleaf. In the matrix below the map, the number of roads used to travel from each town to each of the others is recorded, and the total noted in the column marked row sum. The town with the lowest total is the most accessible because it needs the fewest roads to reach the others. ▷ node, link.

Accessibility is an important factor for shops when choosing a location. Within *shopping centres, the richer chain stores choose the most accessible sites, and out-of-town supermarkets have developed because they are easily accessible by car. ✍

acid With a low *pH. When fuels are burned, among other things they can release compounds of sulphur and nitrogen. These react with rain-water to form **acid rain (acid precipitation)**, which is rain containing sulphuric and nitric acid strong enough to damage vegetation as well as some of the life in streams and lakes, since it also

Accessibilty

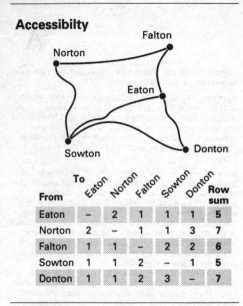

From	To Eaton	Norton	Falton	Sowton	Donton	Row sum
Eaton	–	2	1	1	1	5
Norton	2	–	1	1	3	7
Falton	1	1	–	2	2	6
Sowton	1	1	2	–	1	5
Donton	1	1	2	3	–	7

releases possibly dangerous minerals from rocks into the water supply. The UK Department of the Environment claims that emissions from power-stations need to be cut by about 80% to stop acid rain.

acre An area of land equal to 4840 square yards, or about 0.4 *hectares.

active volcano A *volcano which is likely to erupt. Examples include Mt. St Helens, USA, and Etna, Sicily.

administration Managing or overseeing. All businesses have managers, as do both local governments and central government. The first two **administer** regions of various sizes; the latter administers a whole state, and states, counties, and the French departments are all examples of **administrative regions**.

advanced economy The economy of a *more developed country, generally defined by per capita GDP over $10 000, and with less than 6% of the work-force in agriculture.

aeolian Carried by the wind. **Aeolian landforms** are *landforms such as *pedestal rocks and *yardangs which have mostly been cut by the action of the wind, and are very common in *deserts. ▷ desert landforms.

aerial photograph A photograph taken from overhead, either from directly above (**vertical aerial photograph**), or at an angle (**oblique aerial photograph**).

afforestation Planting trees. Trees may be planted to provide timber, but they can also help to stop *soil erosion, store carbon dioxide, and conserve water. ▷ deforestation.

aftershock A further trembling of the ground which can occur some time after an *earthquake.

age dependency The need of those who are too young or too old to have a job to be supported financially by those who are in work (the *economically active). As a greater number of people in the *more developed countries are living longer and longer beyond retirement age, age dependency may become a problem, since there may not be enough wage-earners to support everyone. In *less developed countries, the problem is the reverse; many LDCs have 50% of their population under 15 years old, but children are also dependent.

Age–sex pyramid

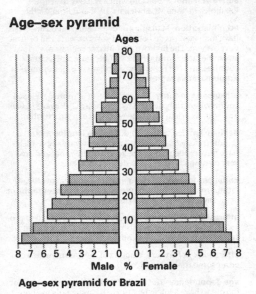

Age–sex pyramid for Brazil

age–sex pyramid A diagram showing the ages and sex of the population of an area. The numbers of people, in five-year age groups, are shown by horizontal bar graphs; usually with males to the left and females to the right. These diagrams are also called *population pyramids.

agglomeration A mass or concentration of something, in one place. In *human geography, this is usually a concentration of *industries or *population.

agrarian Relating to the land, particularly to systems of *land tenure. **Agrarian reform** generally refers to *land reform.

agribusiness A business involved in producing farm goods, and storing, processing, and selling them. It is run very much on business lines, and farming methods are usually *intensive. Managers, and not farmers, decide what to grow, and where, and agribusinesses work on a very large scale. Many operate in several countries and have a turnover of billions of dollars a year.

agricultural policy The programme set out by a government, or group of governments, to steer agriculture in the direction thought best.

agriculture Using the land to grow crops and to rear animals. ▷ Commercial agriculture, subsistence agriculture, extensive agriculture, intensive agriculture.

aid A form of help, usually given from the people of a *developed country to those of a *less developed country. Aid may be in the form of skilled people, training staff, food and medicine, gifts, loans or credits. It may be given by charities (NGOs) or by governments. **Tied aid** is aid given by governments under certain conditions; often that the receiving government agrees to buy some of the donor's goods.

air freight Cargo carried on aircraft. Since air freight rates are high, it is more often the valuable, lighter, or perishable goods that are carried by air.

air mass A large part of the *atmosphere, perhaps hundreds of kilometres across, of similar temperature and moisture content throughout. Air masses move across the earth's surface, bringing with them different types of weather. *Fronts occur where two different air masses meet.

air pressure Also known as **atmospheric pressure**, this is the weight of the *atmosphere as it presses down on to the earth's surface. Air presses down more when it is cold, and therefore heavy, or when it is being forced down and warmed.

algal bloom A dense spread within a river, lake, or sea of the tiny water plants known as **algae**. It can happen if the water is polluted, or gets warmer. ▷ eutrophication.

alluvium Any material laid down by a river, but usually the finer, fertile deposits, which are also called **silt**. Each time the lower course of the river floods, it drops alluvium over the valley floor, eventually forming a *floodplain, such as the floodplain of the Thames. When a river flowing

Alluvial fan

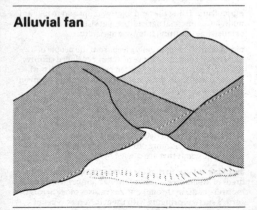

down a steep gradient meets a sudden flattening of the slope, it may deposit a conical wedge of alluvium known as an **alluvial fan**. These fans are often found in *arid regions, where they are formed as a result of *flash flooding.

alp This word can be used for any gently sloping land rising above the steep sides of a *glaciated valley, not just in the Alps. The alp is often used as summer pasture. ▷ glaciated features, transhumance.

alternative power Any power source, such as wind power, using *renewable, rather than *non-renewable resources.

altitude Height, elevation.

alto- Part of a cloud name, describing a cloud at any height between 3000 and 6000 m. **Alto-stratus** are thin, grey layer clouds which make the sun look white. **Alto-cumulus** are white and grey blobs of cloud.

amenity Pleasantness. In geography, the word is used to cover those things, like good housing, open space, and leisure services, which make a place agreeable to live in or to visit. ▷ psychic income. The term **amenity resources** may also be used to describe them.

anemometer An instrument for recording wind speed. A simple **vane anemometer** consists of three cups fixed sideways on to a spindle. The wind blows the cups round, and the speed is shown on a dial. The instrument should be 10 m above ground level.

annotated sketch map A *sketch map with labelling to highlight certain important features. To draw an annotated sketch map, select only the features you wish to highlight. You need not trouble with a scale, and shapes, distances, and directions need only be approximate. It is a good idea to illustrate an examination answer with a sketch map when it will help make a point *even if you are not asked to do so.* ▷▷ sketch map.

annual Each year. An **annual total** gives the amount of something recorded over a year; the **annual range** is the difference between the highest and lowest temperatures recorded in the space of one year. ▷ diurnal.

Antarctic Describing areas south of the **Antarctic circle**; that is, the line of latitude at 66° 30' S. South of this line, winter nights are long, and the sun does not rise at all on 21 June (remember that winter in the Southern Hemisphere is in the European summer). In summer, it is the days which are long, and there is no night on 21 December.

anticline An upwards bend in the *strata, or layers, of folded rock. ▷▷ fold.

anticyclone An area of high pressure (*air pressure) which usually brings fine, settled weather; hot and dry in summer, and cold in winter. Some winter anticyclones cause dry and gloomy weather. Fog may occur. ✍

anti-natalist Opposed to high *birth rates. Many anti-natalist *Third World governments try to keep family sizes small by encouraging contraception.

AONB *Area of Outstanding Natural Beauty.

apartheid The South African system, now in theory no longer operating, of having separate facilities and living spaces for Blacks, Coloureds, and Whites.

appropriate technology The methods and equipment best suited to the incomes and abilities of the people who are to use them. This term is usually used when discussing the most suitable technology for *developing countries where, for example, a number of wells with pumps would be cheaper to make and easier to manage than a massive reservoir and miles of pipes. ▷ intermediate technology.

Anticyclone

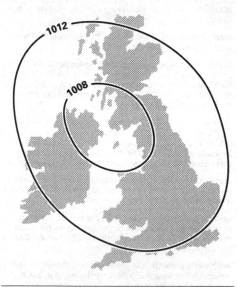

aquifer A rock which will hold water. Boreholes can be drilled into the rock in order to take out the water. ▷▷ artesian basin.

arable Concerned with crops, as in **arable farming** and **arable land**.

arch A natural arch through a cliff or headland, formed when two or more caves, which have been cut on either side of the cliff by the sea, finally join up. In time, the roof of the arch will collapse, leaving a *stack. ▷▷ marine features.

archipelago A group of islands, for example, the Greek islands in the Aegean Sea.

Arctic Describing areas north of the **Arctic Circle**; that is, the line of latitude at 66° 30' N. North of this line, summer nights are short, and the sun does not set at all on 21 June. In winter, it is the days which are short, and there is no daylight on 21 December.

Area of Outstanding Natural Beauty About 6% of England and Wales has been classed as of 'Outstanding Natural Beauty'. In these areas, any proposed development is looked at very carefully by the *planning authorities to make sure it does not spoil the beauty of the landscape. ✍

arête A steep-sided, narrow ridge separating two *corries in a glacially eroded, mountainous region. ▷▷ glacial erosion.

arid Dry—usually with less than 250 mm of rain each year. Some arid areas have more rain, but *evaporation rates are so high that much of the water is lost. **Aridity** is a state of dryness.

arithmetic growth Any growth in quantity where the amount of increase is the same each time, as in 2, 4, 6, 8 . . . or 3, 6, 9, 12 . . . . ▷ Malthus.

arithmetic mean A number representing the average value of any set of figures. To find the mean

(i) Add up all the statistics in the data set.
(ii) Divide this total by the number of statistics. See also median, mode.

Areas of Outstanding Natural Beauty

Ⓐ Lincolnshire Wolds

Ⓑ Chilterns

Ⓒ Wessex Downs

Ⓓ North Downs

Ⓔ South Downs

Ⓕ Bodmin Moor

▓ National parks

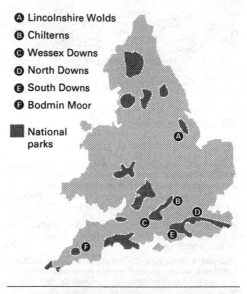

A road In the Department of Transport classification, a major road which is not a *motorway.

artesian Providing water at the surface without the need for pumping it. An **artesian basin** is a wide, gently folded syncline where a *permeable rock, such as chalk, is sand-

Artesian

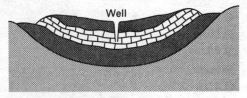

Well

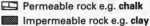

▭ Permeable rock e.g. **chalk**
▮ Impermeable rock e.g. **clay**

---

wiched between layers of *impermeable rock, such as clay. Rainwater soaks into the permeable rock (*aquifer) and, in a true artesian basin, will rise naturally up a borehole drilled down to the central section of the aquifer, because it is under pressure from the *groundwater at the edges of the basin. The London Basin was an artesian basin, but so much water has been extracted from it that the pressure is no longer strong enough to bring water to the surface without pumping.

artificial Man-made; made from minerals. Thus, **artificial fertilizers**, which generally contain one or more of nitrogen, phosphorus, and potassium compounds, are made from petroleum and other mineral deposits, whereas *organic fertilizers such as manure or compost come from remains of currently living organisms. Similarly, **artificial fibres** (man-made fibres), such as nylon or polyester, are made from minerals.

ash *volcanic ash.

aspect The direction in which a slope or valley side faces. In Europe, for example, slopes with a south-facing aspect are sunnier and warmer than north-facing slopes.

assembly industry An industry which puts together parts produced elsewhere to make a finished product. Many *developing countries have a high proportion of this type of industry; components for computers, for example, may be made in Europe but assembled in South-East Asia, where the labour is cheaper. Compare with *manufacturing industry.

assisted area A region which is being helped by the government. ▷development area.

asylum *political asylum.

asymetrical fold A section of upfolded rock *strata where the angles of the *limbs (the downslopes each side of the highest point) are different. ▷▷ fold.

atmosphere The cloak of air, about 100 km in thickness, which encircles the world. The part of the atmosphere we live in is the **troposphere**, which is about 16 km high at the equator and 9 km at the poles. Most of our weather happens within the troposphere. The atmosphere is about 79% nitrogen, 20% oxygen, and 0.03% carbon dioxide (but see global warming). Increasingly, through **atmospheric pollution**, it also contains gases produced by man, such as *sulphur dioxide, *nitrogen oxides, and CFCs which are harmful.

atomic power *nuclear power.

attrition The wearing away of particles of debris, such as gravel, sand, or pebbles, as they bump against each other while being carried along by sea or river water, wind, or glacier ice. Fragments which have been shaped in this way are generally more or less rounded.

automated Using machinery, sometimes 'robots', rather than human labour.

avalanche A mass of material, usually of snow (but rock avalanches do occur), sliding very rapidly down a slope.

axis, earth's A line joining the North and South Poles, around which the earth rotates once roughly every 24 hours.

B

backwash The flow of water back down a beach after a wave has broken. ▷swash.

balance of payments The sum left when the total value of a state's *imports is taken away from the total value of a state's *exports. When the value of the imports is greater the country has a **negative balance of payments**—this can lead to many *economic problems, such as its currency being worth less.

bar A low ridge of sand, slightly out to sea, and usually running parallel to the shore. Bars sometimes run across river mouths and bays (**bay bars**), or can cut off a *lagoon. They are often visible at low tide. ▷marine deposition.

barchan A half-moon-shaped desert dune. A barchan usually has its 'back' to the wind, with its 'horns' extending downwind. Barchans can move downwind by as much as 15 m a year. ▷▷desert features.

bar graph A way of illustrating data by drawing a series of bars in proportion to the totals of the different features shown. *Make sure you draw in a side scale and label each column.* Compare with *histogram. ✐

barograph A type of *barometer which records *atmospheric pressure as an ink line on a paper trace.

barometer An instrument for measuring *atmospheric pressure. A **mercury barometer** shows pressure changes as the height of an upright thread of mercury in a glass tube varies; the weight of the atmosphere pushes the thread of mercury up from the bottom. An **aneroid barometer** is powered by a metal box, containing very

Bar graph

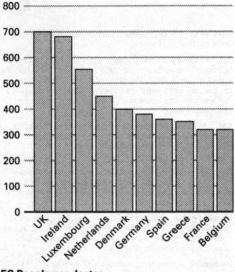

EC People per doctor

little air. As pressure varies, the sides of the box expand and contract, and these changes show up on a dial.

barrage A low dam built across a wide stretch of water, such as a large *estuary, in order to use the water held behind it, perhaps to make electricity. Barrages have been proposed across the Severn and Mersey estuaries. ▷dam, wave power.

basalt A very fine-grained, *igneous rock, formed from lava welling up from volcanoes. It forms most of the sea bed, and a series of basalt flows over land can form a **lava plateau**, such as the Snake Plateau of the USA, which stretches over thousands of square kilometres. Basalt often cracks into hexagonal columns as it cools; the most famous example being the Giant's Causeway, Co. Antrim, Northern Ireland. It *weathers into fertile soil.

baseflow The flow of a river which is fed only by *ground-water. ▷▷hydrograph.

base level The level at which a river reaches a lake or the sea. It cannot cut its bed lower than base level. ▷▷graded profile.

basin An area of land, or of rock *strata, dipping from every side into the middle. A **basin of internal drainage** is one where all the streams flow into the middle, often forming a lake. The water evaporates out, frequently leaving behind flat, salty areas. The Dead Sea, Israel, is an example.

bastee Also known as a **bustee**, this is the Indian term for a *shanty town.

batholith A large volume of *igneous rock, forced up into the earth's *crust by *magma from the *mantle below. Because the magma cools slowly, it forms rocks with large crystals, such as *granite. If the rocks above are eroded away, the batholith will be revealed at the surface; Dartmoor is an example of this. ▷▷intrusion.

bay Part of the sea filling a wide-mouthed opening in the coastline. A **bay bar** is a bar cutting off much of the bay, and is formed by *longshore drift. ▷▷marine features.

beach A strip of *marine sediment deposited along the coastline by the action of waves and *longshore drift. The deposits vary in size from pebbles to sand, and are often sorted by size, with the larger particles at the top of the beach, although it is common to have beaches made entirely of sand or entirely of shingle. The larger the beach material, the steeper the slope of the beach towards the sea. Above the limit of normal high tides, there may be a ridge of larger pebbles and boulders, thrown up during storms. This is the **storm beach**.

Bearing

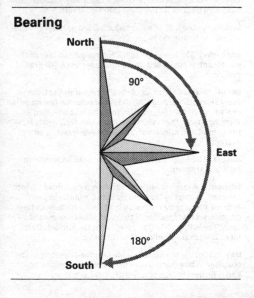

bearing The compass direction from one point to another. It is taken as from North, and always in a clockwise direction. Thus, North is 0°, East 90°, South 180°, and so on. ✍

Beaufort scale A scale of wind speeds, running from 0—calm to 12—*hurricane. The ones you will hear of most often are the gales:

Force 7	Moderate gale	Whole trees move	51–61 km/hr
Force 8	Fresh gale	Twigs snap off	62–74 km/hr
Force 9	Strong gale	Buildings damaged	75–86 km/hr
Force 10	Whole gale	Trees uprooted	87–101 km/hr
Force 11	Storm	Widespread damage	102–15 km/hr
Force 12	Hurricane	Devastation	116+ km/hr

bed A layer of *sedimentary rock which is distinctive in some way. **Bedding** is the arrangement of beds in a rock, and a **bedding plane** separates the beds.

bedload The material bounced or rolled along the river bottom.

Bergschrund

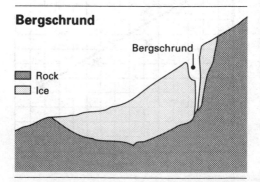

Bergschrund

▨ Rock
☐ Ice

bedrock The solid rock which lies under the soil.

behavioural geography A type of geography which studies the interactions between man and the way he *sees* the environment. This is different from customary geography, which studies the interactions between man and the way the environment actually *is*. For example, an Indian of the Amazon forests will see the rain forest as a home and a source of everyday needs; a Brazilian cattle baron would see the rain forest as something to be cleared so that he

Best-fit line

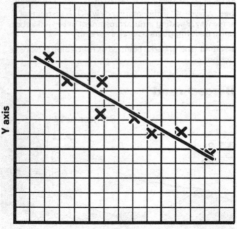

can provide pasture for his animals. Behavioural geography looks at the different ways we all perceive our environment, and how we react to that perception.
▷ landscape evaluation, mental map, perception.

bergschrund A deep crack, or *crevasse, at the head of a corrie glacier. The crevasse is formed as the ice pulls away downslope. ✍

berm A ridge of *sand or shingle on a beach, roughly parallel to the water line, and formed by wave action.

best-fit line A line, usually but not always a straight line, drawn through the points on a *scatter diagram, and constructed to pass as close to all the points as possible. ▷ correlation. ✍

beta index A measurement of how well settlements in a *network are connected to each other (*connectivity). For the whole network, the number of settlements (*nodes) is divided by the number of routes (*links) between them. This index can be used to compare the connectivity of different networks. ✍

Beta index

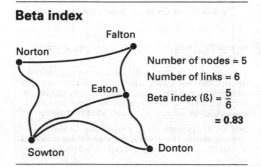

Number of nodes = 5

Number of links = 6

Beta index (ß) = $\dfrac{5}{6}$

= **0.83**

Bid rent

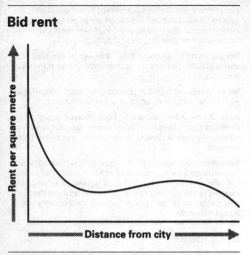

bidonville A French term for a shanty town. ▷shanty town, bastee, favela.

bid rent The rental value of land, whether farm- or built-up land. **Bid-rent theory** assumes that, in a city, rental values are highest at the centre, dwindling as you go out, and then picking up again in the suburbs. A graph showing changes in bid rent over distance is a **bid-rent curve**. 🖎

biofuel Any gaseous, solid, or liquid *fuel formed from *organic matter. The term **biogas** refers to carbon dioxide and methane made from plant and animal wastes; *renewable resources.

biological weathering. The breaking down of rocks *in situ* (without moving them) by living things, such as lichens, tree roots, and burrowing animals. ▷chemical weathering, mechanical weathering.

biosphere The zone of the earth which contains life; from about 3 m below the ground to about 30 m above it, and to a depth of some 200 m below the surface of the sea.

birth rate The number of births in a year per thousand people. Typical rates for a *developed country are 12 ; for a *less developed country, 25 to 35. This comes about because people in less developed countries cannot be sure that all their children will survive, need the help that children's work will give, and have no one to support them in their old age other than their children. As a country goes through the *demographic transition, birth rates fall.

bituminous coal The type of coal used in most *thermal power-stations. It is of medium quality, but contains many pollutants, especially sulphur, and gives off sulphur dioxide when it is burnt. This is one cause of *acid rain.

blast furnace A closed fireplace with an extra oxygen supply, where coke is burned to a temperature high enough to extract pure iron from iron *ore.

bloc A group of countries, held together by some system of politics or trade.

block diagram A drawing, usually of *landforms, designed to give a 3-D impression.

block faulting When many vertical or diagonal *faults occur, the earth's *crust is cut into a series of **blocks**. These may rise or fall in relation to each other. Uplifted blocks form **block mountains**, such as Mt. Ruwenozori (Tanzania), otherwise known as horsts. Sunken blocks form *rift valleys. ▷▷fault.

blowhole A crack running from the bottom to the top of a cliff, which air and sea water rush through, spraying out at the top. ▷ marine erosion.

blue-collar worker Someone in a *manual job, or one where there is a possibility of getting dirty.

blue ice Ice at the base of a glacier which has been so crushed down by the weight of ice above that all the air has been squeezed out, changing its colour from white to blue.

bluff A steep, often vertical section of a river bank, commonly found on the outer bend of a *meander, and also known as a *river cliff. ▷▷ river features.

boss A small *batholith, a few square kilometres in area.

boulder clay An old-fashioned name for *till. It takes its name from the characteristic mixture of large stones, or boulders, and finer *clays found in till.

boundary Any line, visible or invisible, which separates one area, region, or country, from another. The limit of a *hinterland or *urban field is a type of boundary, as is a *frontier.

bourne An intermittent stream in a *dry valley. Whether it flows at all, or where it starts when it does flow, depends on how high the *water-table is. ▷▷ escarpment.

BP Before the present day; a term used in geological dating.

braided channel A river which has split into many streams which wander around bars and temporary islands, only to reform as a single channel. **Braiding** is common when the amount of water in a river varies a great deal, so that it cannot always carry its *load. ▷▷ river features.

break-of-bulk point A place, such as a port, where a cargo is unloaded and broken up into smaller units for further delivery. Although shifting the goods from one transporter to another costs money, it makes sense to keep the whole cargo together for as long as possible. It is also sound sense to process a raw cargo before it moves on from the break-of-bulk point.

break of slope The place where a slope clearly changes angle, becoming much steeper or flatter.

breakwater A wall, running across a beach from the landward end, built to stop the movement of beach material. ▷ longshore drift.

breccia Any rock made of sharp fragments of different types of stone, naturally cemented together.

bridging point Any place where a river is crossed by a bridge. Many towns have grown up at bridging points—Oxford is one. A **lowest bridging point** is the last bridge over a river before it reaches the sea, like Southampton, and can therefore be an important *route centre.

B road In the Department of Transport classification, a road of less importance, and often narrower, than a major, *A road.

bulk transport Carrying one type of cargo in very large quantities, in a transporter, like a juggernaut or supertanker, both of which can be called **bulk carriers**.

Burgess model A *model of the layout of the city which shows the city formed of a series of circular zones, one beyond another. Each zone has a different *function. ▷ sector model, multiple nuclei model.

bush In Australia, the outback, in Africa, the forest or *savanna. **Bush-fallowing** is a method of *subsistence farming, used in the tropics. A patch of forest is cleared, and the trees burnt on the spot—the ash gives some of the

Burgess model

I	Loop
IIa	Factory zone
IIb	Zone in transition
IV	Zone of working men's houses
V	Residential zone

---

*plant nutrients to the soil. Crops are grown on the patch for as long as 5 years, but the soil quickly becomes infertile, and the land is then left to recover for as long as possible. This system requires a lot of land per head, and with

population numbers rising rapidly in this century, too
often the land is used again before it has recovered.
▷ shifting cultivation.

business park An out-of town development combining
offices and light industry, often of the *high-technology
variety. Many business parks are landscaped, with a good
deal of open space. ▷ science park.

bustee *bastee.

butte In *arid areas, like the western United States, a
small, flat-topped, steep-sided hill, made of horizontal
rock *beds and topped by a protective cap of hard rock.
▷ desert features.

buttress root A root which rises above ground level for
part of its length, probably in order to support a very tall
tree. ▷ tropical rain forest.

bypass A road built around, or to one side of a town, in
order to keep traffic out of the town centre.

C

caldera A crater at the mouth of a *volcano, as much as 7 km across, formed when the top of the *cone fell in, perhaps because the *lava drained away, or because the top blew off. Calderas sometimes contain *crater lakes. ▷ volcano ▷▷ volcanic features.

caliper A double-pointed compass, used to measure distances on a map.

calorie A unit of heat. In terms of food, it is a unit of its energy value. People's daily calorie needs vary, but very many people in the *Third World do not eat enough to give them the calories they need; they are *undernourished.

canyon A steep-sided, deep valley, which has developed in an *arid region where the river is the main eroding force and there is very little erosion of the valley sides, because the climate is so dry. An example is the Grand Canyon, on the Colorado River, USA.

CAP Common Agricultural Policy.

capital In economics, all the necessary items for producing wealth, such as machinery, buildings, as well as money. **Capital intensive** techniques, like *market gardening or *automated factories are very productive because they need heavy **capital investment** in equipment.

capital city The centre of government of a state.

capitalist agriculture *Cash cropping based on heavy *capital investment, with high levels of productivity and much of the output sold as *exports. Capitalist agriculture is the norm in the *North, and increasingly common in

*Third World countries, such as Côte d'Ivoire. The underlying motive for capitalist agriculture is profit, rather than, for example, the provision of jobs.

cap rock A layer of hard rock at the top of a feature such as *mesa, *zeugen, or *waterfall.

cargo Any transported *goods.

carnivore A meat-eater. ▷▷ food chain

carrying capacity The maximum number of inhabitants which can be supported in a given area, or country. The term can be used for animals, but in geography is more often used for people. It is difficult to be precise about carrying capacities, because it is difficult to define the term 'support'; there is no real agreement on minimum living standards to show that an individual is adequately supported.

cartel An arrangement between a number of producers to hold a price, and not to compete too strongly with each other. The *Organization of Petroleum Exporting Countries is an example of a cartel.

case study A real-life example of a general principle taught in *human geography.

cash crop A crop grown for sale rather than for *subsistence. The economies of many *Third World countries are dominated by the export of cash crops, such as cocoa or cotton. Unfortunately, prices of export crops are controlled by the *more developed countries. In addition, concentrating on growing cash crops has led to a fall in the production of food crops.

catchment area **1.** In *human geography, the area around a city which the city caters for, or any area served by a particular function, such as a school catchment area. **2.** In *physical geography, a *drainage basin.

cave An opening within a rock. Many **sea caves** are formed when the *erosive power of the sea takes advantage of lines of weakness, such as *faults or *joints to wear away the rock. ▷▷ marine erosion, karst.

cavern A large cave. The largest caverns are found in the limestone country known as *karst.

CBD *Central Business District.

census A survey of the population of a state or region. The UK census is taken every ten years and includes questions, for example, on birthplace, age, sex, jobs, housing, family size, and qualifications. Governments need censuses to plan for the future, and local **census returns** can be found in main libraries. ▷ enumeration district.

Central Business District (CBD) The heart of the city, usually found where the main routes meet, so that it is very *accessible, and largely made up of shops, services, and offices. Since *bid-rents are high, high-rise buildings are common so that land can be used more *intensively. The **CBD** of London consists of the West End and the City.

centrality The extent to which a *central place provides *goods and *services for its population and surrounding area. This depends on the *accessibility of the town as well as on the number of shops. A settlement with a high **centrality index** is accessible, with many available goods and services.

central place Any *settlement providing *goods and/or *services. **Central place theory**, first outlined by Christaller, suggests that settlements form some kind of pattern on the map, with many small, *low-order centres, and progressively fewer, *higher-order centres. It also suggests that settlements of the same size are spaced at regular intervals.

cereal A grain crop, such as wheat, barley, maize, or rice.

Central Place

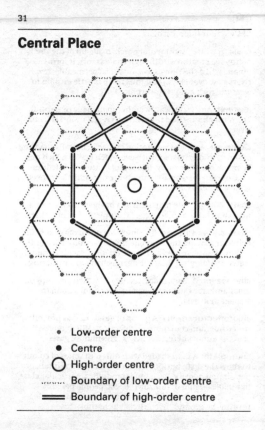

- • Low-order centre
- ● Centre
- ○ High-order centre
- .... Boundary of low-order centre
- ══ Boundary of high-order centre

CFC *chlorofluorocarbon.

chalk A white, *sedimentary rock, made up of the shells of tiny sea creatures. Although chalk is soft, it forms uplands, like the Downs, because it is *permeable; few rivers flow over chalk, and thus there is little erosion to wear the rock away. ▷ escarpment.

channel Any waterway, whether man-made or natural. The term **channelled flow**, however, generally refers to rivers.

chaparral A type of vegetation characteristically made up of short, woody bushes, with evergreen leaves which may be thick, hairy, or shiny. It is found in areas of *Mediterranean climate where summers are dry, and plants need to save water. ▷ maquis.

chart A large-scale map such as a navigation chart, or a map showing a small range of features. ▷ synoptic chart.

chemical weathering The breaking down of rocks *in situ* (without moving them) by chemical reactions, such as the action of water, of oxygen in the air, or of *acids in rainwater. ▷ biological weathering, mechanical weathering .

chernozem A deep, black, fertile soil which develops on grassland areas such as the prairies of Canada and the steppes of Russia.

chlorofluorocarbons A group of gases used as propellant in aerosols and coolant in refrigerators. When released into the atmosphere, they act as *greenhouse gases.

choropleth A map shaded with different tones of colour to show the distribution of some feature, like rainfall, or population density. Each tone stands for a particular class, like 250–500 mm of rain, or 100–200 people per km². Often, the darker the shading is, the more dense the feature on the ground. To construct a choropleth:

Chloropleth

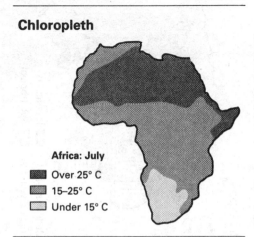

Africa: July

■ Over 25° C
▨ 15–25° C
□ Under 15° C

(i) Decide on the limits of each type of shading, for example 0–20, 21–30, 31–40, and so on . . .
(ii) Decide on how to shade the map, following the guidelines given above.
(iii) Fill in each area with the relevant shading, making sure that there are no 'breaks' between two regions of the same shading.
(iv) Add a title and a key.

cirque *corrie.

cirro-, cirrus Words used to describe the high, wispy clouds sometimes called mares' tails. When the skies are clear, the appearance of cirrus can indicate that there is a *depression on the way. ▷▷ cloud types.

Some important climatic types

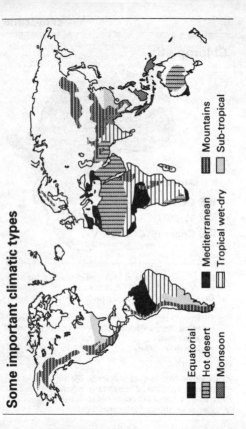

Equatorial Hot desert Monsoon

Mediterranean Tropical wet-dry

Mountains Sub-tropical

city A large *urban, *central place which provides *high-order, quite specialized goods and services. There is no set population figure at which a settlement becomes a city. In the UK, any central place with a cathedral is a city, but this is an unusual definition.

clay A soil made of very small particles—under 0.02 mm across. There are almost no air spaces in clay; this makes it very heavy, and it quickly becomes waterlogged in the wet. For these reasons, farmers have often left clay soils as pasture, or have added lime to make them easier to cultivate. ▷marl.

cliff A steep rock wall, usually facing the sea. Cliffs form best in resistant rocks, like the granite cliffs of Hoy, Orkney Islands, but Britain's most famous cliffs—the white cliffs of Dover—are of chalk. (For an explanation, see chalk.) *Marine erosion may cut *caves, *arches, and *stacks in cliffs.

climate The average pattern of weather throughout the year for any particular region, rather than the weather on one particular day. It has been said, half jokingly, that Britain does not have a climate, since the summers, for example, are so difficult to predict.

climatic To do with *climate. A **climatic region** is an area where the climate is more or less the same throughout; an area which has the same **climatic type**.   ✎

climatic change Climates change over time; Britain in the eighteenth century, for example, had colder winters than we do (see *Little Ice Age). Changes may be due to variations in the orbit of the earth around the sun, the tilt of the earth, or the outpouring of ash from volcanoes. It is possible that all the climates of the earth will change as a result of the increased discharges of *greenhouse gases.

Clinometer

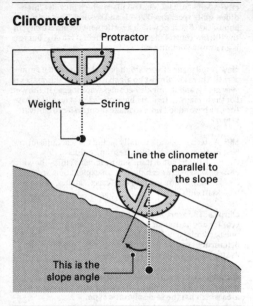

Protractor

Weight — String

Line the clinometer parallel to the slope

This is the slope angle

clinometer An instrument used to measure the angles of a slope. They can be expensive, but a home-made clinometer can be easily made, and gives reasonable results.

clint A slab in a *limestone pavement, usually separated from others by *grykes. ▷ karst.

cloud A dense mass of water droplets and/or ice crystals, visible in the sky. The higher the cloud, the more ice it will contain. Clouds generally form when air rises, perhaps because of convection, or because the air is forced up over higher ground, so that the water vapour it contains cools and *condenses. **Cloud types** are classed by their height: *cirrus (high level, over 6000 m) and *altus (medium level, 3000–6000 m), and also by their shape: *cumulus (rather like a cauliflower) and *stratus (in a layer). There is a regular sequence of cloud types as a *depression approaches and passes over.   ✍

coal A sedimentary rock, formed from the vegetation of tropical swamps which existed some 300 million years ago, and has since been naturally compressed and hardened. In the late eighteenth and nineteenth centuries, coal power was vital to industry, so that most of Britain's industry grew up in coalfield areas. With increased use of electricity, and falling demand for coal, most coal-mines have closed, and coalfields, like that in South Wales, have become *depressed areas.

coast The boundary between the land and the sea.

coastal At, or near, the *coast. **Coastal marsh** is low-lying waterlogged ground with plants, like reeds, which can tolerate salty conditions, and can be the result of a *spit cutting off a *lagoon, which then is filled with river *silt. A **coastal plain** is a belt of lowland bordering the coast and **coastal shipping** refers to ships which move from port to port along the coast.

coking coal Coal with a high carbon, and low water content; the type used in *blast furnaces. When large amounts of coking coal were needed to make iron and steel, blast furnaces were usually sited on coalfields. Much less coal is now needed, so that today a coalfield site is less important for iron making.

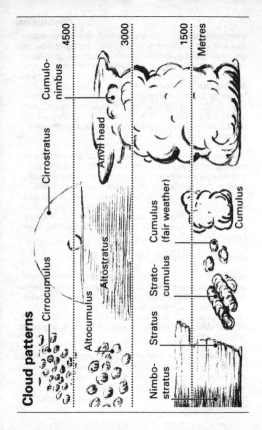

cold anticyclone An area of high pressure caused by a mass of cold, heavy air. It generally brings fine, very cold weather. **cold front** The border of a mass of cold air as it moves over towards a region. ▷ front, depression.

colliery A coal-mine.

collision A pile-up. A zone where *plates **collide** is a *destructive margin.

colonialism The conquering and controlling of one or more territories by a foreign power. In the late nineteenth century, for example, all of Africa except Ethiopia and Liberia was ruled by European states, known as **colonial powers**. Although most colonies are now independent states, **colonial influence** is strong, both in their systems of government and in their economies. ▷ neo-colonialism.

commercial agriculture Agriculture producing goods which are for sale, rather than for *subsistence.

commodities Goods, materials for sale.

common land Land which belongs to no one, and therefore to everyone; anyone may use it. There is still some common land left in Britain, mostly in village greens and a few upland areas.

communications The connections and links that people use. These include railways, roads, and waterways, posts, telephones, faxes, radios, and newspapers.

community A group of people living in a distinctive area, such as a *neighbourhood. The local issues which may concern them, like the opting out of the local school or the building of a new factory in the area, can be called **community politics**, and the *facilities shared by the community can be called **communal**.

commuter Anyone who travels some distance to work, most frequently from *suburbs or villages into a city. **Commuting** is usually on a daily basis, but can occur weekly, and most large *urban areas are ringed by **commuter zones** from where many of the residents **commute**. ▷Burgess model, dormitory town.

compass A device used in navigation. A swivelling magnetic needle indicates north, and **compass *bearings** can be taken from north to show the direction in which to travel to the desired destination.

Compass rose

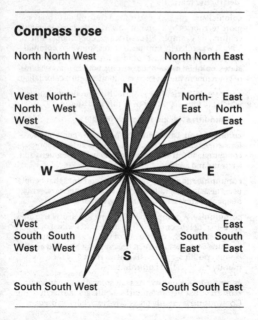

North North West

North North East

West North-
North West
West

North- East
East North
East

N

W

E

West
South South
West West

East
South South
East East

S

South South West

South South East

compass directions can be shown on a **compass rose** (see illustration). ✍

competition 1. In business, one organization producing a good or service which another organization also produces. In theory, competition keeps prices lower, but see *cartel. **2.** In *human geography a contest for the use of land. ▷bid-rent, land use conflict.

compost pit A *dry farming technique used in West Africa. Pits about 1 m wide are dug, and filled with compost. The scanty rain gathers in the pits, where it is absorbed by the compost. This technique makes the most of low annual rainfall.

computer simulation A computer programme designed to recreate actual events as closely as possible. From this it may be possible to predict future events, such as the likely consequences of earthquakes in California or of unchecked world population growth. The more information the computer has, the more accurate the predictions should be.

concealed coalfield A coalfield where the seams of coal are at some depth below the ground surface—in the Yorks, Derby, and Nottingham coalfield, coal has been mined at a depth of 800 m. ▷exposed coalfield.

concealed unemployment Unemployment figures are based on the number of people who register as unemployed. Those people without jobs who do not sign on, perhaps because they know that no jobs are available, make up concealed unemployment.

concentric model *Burgess model.

concordant coastline A coastline parallel to the trend of the mountains directly inland from the coast; also known as a Pacific coastline. When such a coastline is *drowned, either because the land sinks or the sea-level rises, a string of islands parallel to the new coastline will be all that is visible of those mountains. The best example is along the eastern coast of the Adriatic Sea. ▷discordant coastline.

condensation The transformation of a vapour into a liquid, usually due to cooling. *Clouds and *fog form when *water vapour **condenses** into droplets.

cone A feature in the landscape which is roughly circular, rising sharply to a point at the centre. The most common feature with this shape is a volcanic cone, or **cone volcano**, like Fujiyama, Japan. Some volcanoes have small **parasitic cones** on their sides. ▷▷volcanic features.

Confederation of Independent States (CIS) The term used to describe the former Soviet Union.

confluence The point at which one stream joins another. ▷▷river features.

coniferous Trees producing cones, such as the pine. **Coniferous forest** consists of *evergreens, such as fir and spruce, with needle-like leaves to cut down water loss through *transpiration. Naturally occurring coniferous forest, like the *taiga, is easy for timber companies to work because the trees grow in pure stands. Increasingly, timber companies are required to replant cut-down areas. ▷sustainable forestry ▷▷natural vegetation.

connectivity In a transport system, the degree to which *central places are directly linked together by routes. Connectivity can be measured using the *beta index.

conservation The care of species, *resources, and *environments so that they will survive for future generations. This does not mean that resources cannot be used; it does mean that we need recycling, careful use of resources, and cutting down on waste, pollution, and the destruction of habitats.

conservation area A built-up area of such outstanding architectural merit that the buildings in it cannot be

altered or demolished without permission, which would
be difficult to get.

conservative margin   In *plate tectonics, a plate boundary where the movement of the plates is side-by-side rather
than up or down. An example is the margin of the north-
moving California plate and south-moving Pacific plate.
The San Andreas fault is a part of this particular conservative margin.

constructive margin   In *plate tectonics, a plate boundary where plates are forced apart by up-welling *magma,
as happens in the mid-Atlantic. It is here that new plate
material is formed.

consumer   Anyone who buys *goods and/or *services.

container   A metal crate of a standard size, large enough
to make up a lorry load, which can be lifted with a crane
on to a ship or train without the need for re-packing. **Con-
tainerization** has cut down on transport handling costs
and speeded up *freight transport. Felixstowe is an example of a specialized **container port**.

continental drift   The theory, suggested in 1915, that all
the present-day continents were joined together, about
200 million years ago, in a supercontinent, known as *Pangaea. This split into two: *Laurasia in the north and *Gondwanaland to the south, and these split into the continents
as we know them now. The theory was doubted because no
one could explain how continents could move, but is now
backed up by the theory of *plate tectonics, which
explains how movement begins at *constructive margins.

continental shelf   An area of shallow sea—less than 200 m
deep—which borders most of a continent. Water is shallow
enough for light to penetrate, and thus for *photosynthesis to take place, so that there is enough plankton and
plant life to support fish. Continental shelves are therefore
good fishing grounds.

contour A line drawn on a map connecting places of the same height above sea-level. The **contour interval** is the vertical spacing between contours; 1 : 50 000 Ordnance Survey maps have a 10 m interval and 1 : 25 000 maps have a 5 m interval. **Submarine contours** show depths below the water-line, and are often shown in *fathoms*—about 2 m. Contours are examples of *isolines.

contour ploughing Ploughing *across* a slope, rather than up and down it; that is, along the contour. This is done to slow down rain-water as it washes down a slope, and thus to cut down *soil erosion. ▷ grass strip.

contract farming Many large food-processing companies make an arrangement for a farmer to grow a certain crop, which they then guarantee to buy at harvest time. The company often supplies the seed and the fertilizers.

conurbation A large, continuous built-up area, made up of many towns. The towns will have grown up separately, as with Walsall, West Bromwich, Wednesbury, and Wolverhampton, but then they expanded until they joined up to form the West Midlands conurbation.

convection The process by which a warm gas or liquid rises. When convection occurs in warm, moist air, the air cools as it rises, and may cool enough for the water vapour to *condense. Rain may then fall; this is known as **convection rain**. 🖎

conventional power-station Almost all electricity is made by rotating a magnet inside a coil of wire, and the magnet is turned by a turbine. In a conventional power-station steam turns the turbines, and the water is heated by burning coal, gas, or oil.

cooling tower A large chimney built as part of a *conventional power-station in order to keep temperatures at a safe, low level.

Convection

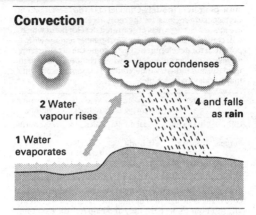

3 Vapour condenses

2 Water vapour rises

4 and falls as rain

1 Water evaporates

co-operative An organization whose members combine their resources in order to make the most of them. Farmers in an **agricultural co-operative** and craftsmen in **trade co-operatives** can buy machinery that they could not afford on their own, and sell their goods in bulk. Co-operatives are found throughout the more developed world—Danish agriculture depends heavily on co-operatives (which also train students)—and the less developed world.

coordinate One of two reference numbers on a graph or map. Used together, the coordinates will pin-point a spot on the graph, or map, as in a *grid reference.

core 1. In *physical geography, the centre of the earth, made of iron and nickel, and very hot. 2. In *human geography, part of the *core–periphery model. A **core region** is a highly *developed region.

core–periphery model A *model of world *development. Certain *core regions are the most developed. Then there are *upward-moving* areas of scattered development which will continue to grow, and *resource-frontier* regions with potential for development. Lastly come the deteriorating *downward-moving* zones, often where resources have been used up, and industry is declining. This model works on many scales, for example:

	Core	Upward-moving	Resource-frontier	Downward-moving
UK	the South-East	East Anglia	Shetlands	the North-East
Europe	*Benelux, Northern Germany	Bavaria	South-West France(?)	Southern Italy
World	Eastern USA	*NICs	Alaska	*LDCs

There are two ways of looking at the core. One is that the core is the centre of new developments, which will eventually filter out to the periphery and help it to develop. The other is that the core attracts most of the investment, and most of the intellectual resources, starving the periphery, and leaving it worse off. This model is often called the Myrdal model, after the man who devised it.

corner shop A local shop, often 'open all hours', where people tend to buy *low-order, convenience goods, often paying slightly more than in a supermarket because it is handy.

corrasion The filing away of a rock as pieces of stone held in river or sea water, *glacier ice, or wind are pounded against it; another word for *abrasion.

correlation A link, or relationship, between two sets of *variables, such as rainfall and crop yields, or intensity of sunshine and incidence of skin cancer. The two sets can be

used as *coordinates to draw a *scatter diagram. If a link
exists between the two groups, it will be possible to draw a
*best-fit line on the scatter diagram. The degree of the link
can be calculated mathematically, by using tests such as
the *Spearman rank-correlation test, which will yield a
correlation coefficient with the following meaning:

Value of correlation coefficient	Meaning
+ 1.0	Perfect positive correlation
+ 0.4 to 0.99	Positive correlations, ranging from weak to very strong
+ 0.4 to − 0.4	No real correlation
− 0.4 to − 0.99	Negative correlations, ranging from weak to very strong
− 1.0	Perfect negative correlation

corridor An arm of one state's territory stretching
through that of another, usually to gain access. An example is the long corridor of Namibia which runs between
Angola and Botswana, giving it access to Zambia and Zim-
babwe.

corrie A roughly circular hollow, cut into solid bedrock.
The side and back walls are steep, but the front opens
downslope. Corries may be up to 2 km across. They are features of *glacial erosion, and will once have contained
corrie glaciers.

corrosion The *erosion which takes place as a liquid dis-
solves a solid. One very common example is the action of
rain- and river-water on limestone. This water contains
some dissolved carbon dioxide, which makes it acidic
enough to dissolve limestone. ▷ karst.

cost–benefit analysis A way of assessing the impact of
any new scheme which takes into account social effects, as
well as economic ones. For example, if a new road is to

spoil the view, as well as speed up the traffic, an attempt is made to put a financial figure on damaging the scenery so that this factor can be put into the sum of profit and loss. Of course, it is very difficult to actually put a cash value on spoiling a beauty spot, but it is an attempt to consider other factors besides purely economic ones.

cottage industry Small-scale industry, like weaving, potting, and forging, which takes place at, or near, the workers' homes.

counter-urbanization The movement of people away from towns and cities. As they grow larger, *urban areas may become less attractive as congestion, air *pollution, and, possibly, crime increases, and many people prefer to live in the country. Counter-urbanization has speeded up with the building of motorways, and as more people are able to work from home, by using faxes and computers, it should quicken even further.

country 1. A loose term for state. 2. *Rural areas.

county town The town where the *administration of a county is, or was, carried out.

cove A small *bay.

cover crop A crop, like sweet potato or dwarf French beans, which tends to sprawl over a field, thus protecting the soil from *erosion. It is especially useful in areas of heavy, tropical rainfall, and is often planted between the rows of another crop.

crag A steep and rugged rock. Some are *arêtes or *truncated spurs.

crag and tail A mass of rock—the *crag—which has lain in the path of a *glacier and protected the softer rock behind it from erosion, so that a long 'tail' stretches beyond the crag.

Crag and tail

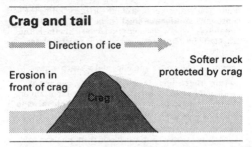

Direction of ice ➡

Softer rock
protected by crag

Erosion in
front of crag

Crag

---

crater A roughly circular opening at the top, or vent, of a
*volcano, often a *caldera. Water may collect here, to form
a **crater lake**. ▷▷ volcanic features.

credit A loan, either of money, goods, or equipment. This
is a common form of *aid to the *Third World.

creek **1.** In the UK, a small inlet of the sea. **2.** In the
USA, a stream. **3.** In Australia, an intermittent stream.

crevasse A wedge-shaped crack in a *glacier, up to 40 m
in depth, caused by strains within the moving ice. **Transverse crevasses** run across the glacier, and occur when the
ice moves down a steep slope. **Longitudinal crevasses**
run parallel with the glacier, and occur when the valley
widens. ▷▷ glacier.

C road In the UK Department of Transport classification,
a minor, often narrow, road.

cross-section In geography, a drawing of a downwards
'slice' through a landscape, or across and through a river,
using the contour lines on a map.

crude oil Mineral oil as it comes out of the ground, before
it is refined.

crust The hard, outer shell of the earth, including the continents, **continental crust**—some 25 to 90 km thick; and the ocean floor, **oceanic crust** 5 to 10 km thick. The crust is divided into sections, known as **crustal plates**. ▷▷ plate.

cuesta A ridge with a *dip slope and a *scarp slope.

culture The customs, beliefs, technology, and arts of a particular people. **Cultural factors** can be important in shaping a landscape, or in giving a different character to areas of a city populated by *ethnic minorities.

culvert A man-made, covered drainage channel. Some are constructed so that rivers can be fed through them to allow building to take place over them (the River Fleet, in Fleet Street, has been **culverted**); others are built to speed up drainage and cut down on *flooding.

cumec A measurement of water flow, standing for *cubic metres per second.* ▷ discharge.

cumulative causation A series of events, each one caused by the one before, and often working in a circle. This can cause a favoured region to become more prosperous:

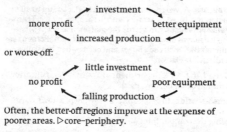

or worse-off:

Often, the better-off regions improve at the expense of poorer areas. ▷ core–periphery.

cumulus A type of cloud, up to 5000 m high, and taller than it is broad, often likened to a cauliflower. **Cumulo-**

stratus are the same thickness, but form a continuous sheet. **Cumulo-nimbus** clouds are much taller—up to 12 000 m. They are commonly known as thunder-clouds, although they need not bring thunder, and have a distinctive, flattened (anvil) head. ▷▷cloud.

cut-off *ox-bow lake.

cwm Welsh for *corrie.

cycle A repeating series of events. **1.** The **cycle of erosion** imagines a landscape which has been lifted up, completely eroded over time to a flat plain, and then lifted up again for further erosion. **2.** The **cycle of poverty** shows how poor states, or poor people, become poorer. There are many versions; here are two:

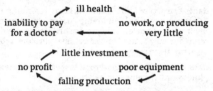

These are both *negative* forms of *cumulative causation.

cyclone An area of very low *atmospheric pressure. A cyclone in Britain will be below 980 millibars (mb). A **tropical cyclone**, with pressure below 970 mb, is more commonly called a *hurricane. Both are associated with stormy weather.

D

dairy A building used for producing and/or keeping milk, butter, and cheese. **Dairying**, or **dairy farming** is the production of milk, usually from cows, but also from sheep and goats. Dairy farming tends to take place near *urban areas, where demand is high, or in areas with mild temperatures and rainfall of over 750 mm per annum. Current EC agricultural policy has led to overproduction of dairy products; the 'butter mountain' is one result.

dam A structure built to hold back water, forming a *reservoir. It may be built to stop flooding, to generate *hydroelectric power, or to provide *irrigation water. The reservoirs may be used for recreational purposes. ▷ barrage, multi-purpose river project.

data Statistics, numbers. Properly speaking, this is a plural word; the singular is **datum**.

death rate The number of deaths per year per thousand people. Death rates are good indicators of *development; a more developed country will have rates of around 12 per thousand, a less developed about 20. (Some less developed countries have surprisingly low rates; this is because as much as 50% of their population is under 18.) The major causes of the fall at the beginning of this century in European and North American death rates were better sanitation, hygiene, and nutrition. ▷ demographic transition model.

debt Anything which is owed, usually money. The **national debt** of a state is the money it owes to private banks and individuals. National debt need not be a problem if the country has the means to repay it, or at least to

pay the *interest. Many *Third World countries are heavily
in debt; in 1988, Côte d'Ivoire's debt, for example, represented 114% of its *GDP. It is **indebtedness** on this scale
which has led to demands for *Western banks to cancel all
or some of **Third World debt** in order to ease the current
debt crisis affecting so much of the *South.

decentralization The movement of people, shops, offices,
and businesses out of the city. The movement may happen
naturally, as people find the city becoming dirty and
crowded, or because of government intervention, as when
the UK government moved the Royal Mint to Llantrisant,
in South Wales. ▷counter-urbanization.

deciduous Describing broad-leaved trees which drop
their leaves in autumn. In freezing winter weather, trees
are unable to take up water. In order to lessen water loss
through *transpiration, deciduous trees shed their leaves.
Deciduous forest is the *natural vegetation of *temperate
regions, producing *hardwood. ▷▷natural vegetation.

deficiency disease A disease caused by a lack of some
essential element in the diet. Some examples are:

Lack of . . .	Deficiency disease
Protein	Kwashiorkor
Iodine	Goitre
Vitamin A	Cataracts
Vitamin B	Beri-beri
Vitamin C	Scurvy
Vitamin D	Rickets

Deficiency diseases are most common in the *less developed countries. Compare with *degeneracy disease. ▷mal-
nutrition.

deflation The removal of loose material by wind. It is
most effective in *desert areas.

deforestation Cutting down trees without replacing
them. Tree roots bind the soil; when the trees have been

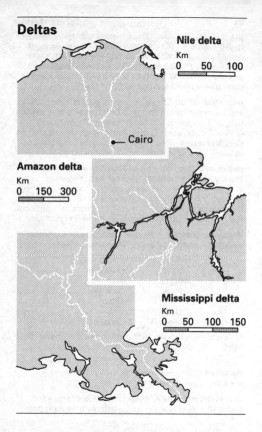

Deltas

Nile delta

Km
0 50 100

Cairo

Amazon delta

Km
0 150 300

Mississippi delta

Km
0 50 100 150

felled, *soil erosion is much more likely. Deforestation in Nepal, mainly for fuel, has been blamed for flooding in Bangladesh, but this is by no means certain. Trees are felled for their timber, or to clear new land for agriculture, and the deforestation and burning of large parts of Amazonia, for example, has released large quantities of the *greenhouse gas, carbon dioxide, into the *atmosphere. ▷ global warming.

degeneracy disease A disease caused by living 'too well'. Eating large amounts of sugar, fat, and refined foods, together with smoking, has been linked with tooth decay, heart disease, and cancer—all degeneracy diseases. Degeneracy diseases are most common in *more developed countries. Compare with *deficiency disease.

delta A low-lying area at the mouth of a river, formed of deposits of *alluvium. *Deposition occurs because the river slows down when it enters a lake or the sea, and cannot carry as much *silt. The Nile has an **arcuate delta**, the Mississippi a **bird's foot delta**, and the Amazon an **estuarine delta**. Delta lands are often very fertile.   ✍

demographic ageing The increase in the average age of a population. By the year 2010, one person in four in the *EC will be over retirement age. This leaves a smaller number of the *economically active to provide for pensions and social security.

demographic transition model A *model of population growth, based on trends in birth and death rates in Europe. Four stages are suggested:

(I)   High, stationary: birth and death rates are high—above 30 per thousand—so that population grows only slowly.

(II) Early expanding: while birth rates remain high, death rates fall to below 15 per thousand, due to improvements in sanitation, diet, and medicine. Population grows dramatically.

(III) **Late expanding:** birth rates now fall as a result of increased prosperity, and better education and job prospects for women. Population continues to grow, but more slowly.

(IV) **Low, stationary:** birth and death rates are now around 12 per thousand. Population grows very slowly; numbers may even fall.

Demographic transition model

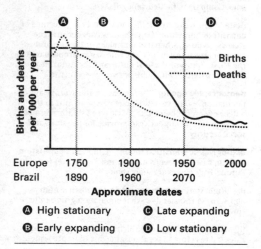

- **A** High stationary
- **B** Early expanding
- **C** Late expanding
- **D** Low stationary

Stages I to IV have been linked with various stages of
*development:

Stage	Development stage	Example
I	Pre-industrial society	Parts of Papua New Guinea
II	*Less developed countries	Kenya
III	*Newly industrializing countries	Brazil
IV	*More developed countries	France

but it is by no means certain that a society at present in
stage I will go through all the other stages.

demography The study of human populations; their
size, *distribution, and composition.

dense Close together. **Densely populated areas** generally have more than 200 people per square km—but this
does not necessarily mean that they are *overpopulated.

density In geography, the average number of some feature, usually people, in a given area; usually in a square
kilometre. ▷ population.

density-shading map Another term for *choropleth.

denudation The wearing away of the earth's surface as a
result of *weathering and *erosion.

depopulation The movement of people out of an area.
▷ rural depopulation.

deposition The dropping of *sediments (load) which have
been carried by water, wind, or ice. The ability of a river,
for example, to carry its load depends on the volume and
speed of flow. ▷ discharge. If either decreases, deposition
will occur. *Glacial deposition occurs when a *glacier
melts; wind-borne sediments are deposited when the wind
drops.

depressed region A region, usually within a *more developed country, where industry is in decline, unemployment is high, and people are moving away. These regions were often once dependent on *heavy industries like iron and steel and shipbuilding which have suffered badly from falling demand and foreign competition. In Britain, parts of the North-East, the North-West, and Central Scotland are depressed regions.

depression An area of low *atmospheric pressure (roughly, below 996 mb). The most common form of depression in Britain results from the meeting of a sequence of a cold, a warm, and a second cold *air mass, with two *fronts separating them. The cold air comes from polar regions; the warm from the *tropics. The first sign of

Depression (1)

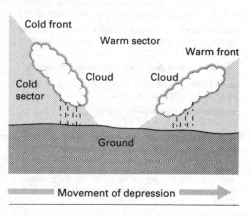

Movement of depression

Depression (2)

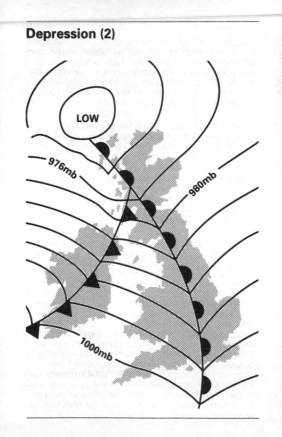

a depression is high, *cirrus cloud. The cloud thickens and lowers, changing from *alto-stratus, to medium-level *stratus, and then to *nimbo-stratus. As the cloud develops, rain falls. Once the warm front arrives, temperatures rise, and the rain generally clears up. This is later followed by the cold front, when there will be more rain, and when temperatures will fall again. ▷ frontal rain. ✍️

derelict Abandoned, unused. Most **derelict land** in Britain is found in the *inner cities, where industry and people have moved out because of cramped, dirty conditions.

desalination The extraction of fresh water from salty sea water. The water is either distilled, which uses a lot of *energy, or filtered through a membrane. Both methods are expensive, but desalination is vital in rich countries with a lack of water, like Kuwait.

desert An *arid area, usually with less than 250 mm of rainfall each year. There is little vegetation, and population *densities are very low. **Hot deserts**, such as the Sahara and Atacama, are found in the tropics, where temperatures may rise to above 50 °C. Here, *aridity mostly comes about because the air is sinking, which makes rainfall unlikely. In addition, the *prevailing winds are *westerly, and drop most of their moisture over cold sea areas offshore. Nights can be as cold as −10 °C, since there is no cloud to stop the heat radiating away. **Temperate deserts**, such as the Gobi, lack rain because they are far from the sea, and the winds that reach them have already dropped their moisture. Summer temperatures are around 20 °C, winters as cold as −20 °C. **Cold deserts** are found in high latitudes—above 60 °. Here the air is too cold to hold much moisture. Summer temperatures are around 15 °C; winters down to −60 °C at times. ▷ tundra, natural vegetation.

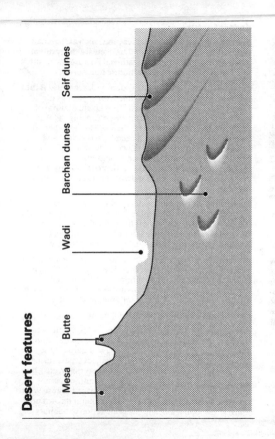

Desert features

Mesa

Butte

Wadi

Barchan dunes

Seif dunes

desert features Most desert features, such as *barchan and *seif dunes, *yardangs, and *zeugen are the result of *wind action, but *wadis and *alluvial fans are the result of rare bursts of short-lived but intense rainstorms. ✍

desertification The spread of *desert-like conditions into the *semi-arid regions, bordering deserts, such as the *Sahel. Many explanations have been given: removal of vegetation due to *overgrazing, *overcropping, *global warming, or natural *climatic change. The remedies are thought to be *dry farming methods, *irrigation, and *afforestation, the addition of water-absorbing plastic grains to the soil, and small-scale methods, such as the use of *diguettes and *grass strips. Rather confusingly, not every specialist believes that desertification is actually taking place.

desire line A straight line drawn on a map to connect the point of origin with a traveller's destination. In theory, the longer the desire line, the higher the order of goods and services at the destination. Desire lines can depict the *catchment area (or *urban field) of a *central place. ✍

destructive margin In *plate tectonics, a plate boundary where plates are forced together. The denser plate slides below the other, as at the margin of the Pacific and Eurasian plates. These margins are associated with *earthquakes, *volcanoes, and *fold mountains. ▷▷ plate.

developing countries See development.

development The use of *resources and technology to improve the *standard of living of a state This definition is based on the gap between the *living standards of the *developed and the *less developed worlds (as expressed, for example, by per capita *GNP, life expectancy, etc.), but it may be that a change to *'Western' conditions is not in the best interests of a *Third World country, because Western development seems also to have brought its own problems: stress, pollution, and the destruction of habitats and

Desire line

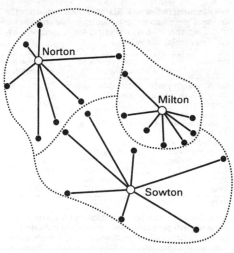

species. **Developing countries** are those which are trying to match Western living standards through development. This is the **development process**, which usually involves *industrialization. Developing countries can be helped in this process by **development assistance**; another term for *aid. ▷development indicators.

development area In Britain, a *depressed area recognized by the government as being in need of help. This help can be in the form of grants, loans, tax agreements, and the supply of factory buildings.

development indicators Statistics used to measure the degree of *development of a country. Below are some indicators, together with typical values for *more developed and *less developed countries:

Indicator	Less developed country (LDC)	More developed country (MDC)
*Infant mortality rate	150/1000 and over	10/1000 or less
Daily *calorie intake	Under 2200	Over 2200
*Literacy rate	c.25%	c.99%
Percentage having secondary schooling	Under 20%	Over 80%
Percentage of workers in agriculture	Over 60%	c.3%
Per capita electricity consumption/year	c.200 kg coal equivalent	c.5000 kg coal equivalent
*Per capita *GNP	Under $3000*	Over $9000*
*Birth rate	Over 30/1000	c.12/1000
*Death rate	Over 15/1000	c.12/1000

*1992.

A run-down of development indicators for a state is its **development profile**. Other development indicators include fertility, *life expectancy, health, *industrialization, and income. Attempts have been made to combine many of these indicators into one measurement. ▷ physical quality of life, Human Development Index.

dew *Precipitation, in the form of moisture condensing out at ground level. **Dew point** is the temperature at which *condensation begins when moist air is cooled. Dew point varies with the amount of water vapour in the air.

differential erosion The uneven erosion of hard and soft rocks; the softer rocks are eroded more rapidly, and the harder rocks then stand out. ▷ cap rock, headland, yardang, zeugen.

diffusion The spreading out of a new invention, technique, or idea, from a centre or centres. This innovation may be anything from an epidemic disease to a political belief. The innovation spreads through in a **diffusion wave**; a 'ripple' of the new element spreading outwards from one place to another.

diguette A low barrier of stones, stalks, and branches, built along a *contour across fields to halt the run-off of rainwater. All that is needed is a cheap spirit-level, and the raw materials, which are found locally. The diguette is a perfect example of *appropriate technology because it is simple and cheap. Diguettes can increase soil levels by 15 to 20 cm over a few years.

dip The slope angle of a rock *stratum from the horizontal. A **dip slope** is the gentler of the two slopes on each side of an *escarpment. (Compare *scarp slope) ▷ folding ▷▷ cuesta.

discharge Shown in the equations as Q, this is the amount of water flowing across the width of a river at a given point. It is measured in *cumecs, and can be calculated as $A \times V$, where A is the area of the *cross-section of the river, and V is the velocity of the river. In the UK, the highest discharges usually come in spring, when water from melted snow is added to normal rainwater. The discharge of major rivers is checked regularly to assess the likelihood of *flooding.

discordant coastline A coastline which cuts across the *folds and *faults of a landscape. When such a coastline is *drowned, either because the land sinks or the sea-level rises, the valleys will be flooded, and *rias or *fiords will form. Compare *concordant coastline.   ✍

dispersed Scattered. **Dispersed settlement** consists of isolated houses and farms, and is normally found in

Discordant coastline of S.W.Eire

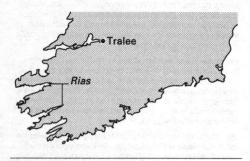

regions of high land, poor soils, or plenty of water.
▷▷ settlement pattern.

distance The space between two points. Distance is usually given in linear units, such as miles or kilometres, but
it can also be stated in terms of time or cost.

distance decay The decreasing effect of anything as you
move away from it. The further people live from a city, for
example, the less they visit it. The term is very similar to
friction of distance.

distributary A river which has branched *away* from the
main river. Distributaries are much rarer than *tributaries*; you will not often see them on an OS map. ▷▷ river
features.

distribution In geography, the way some feature, such as
population, or woodland, is spread over the landscape. To
describe a distribution, use geographical directions—

north, north-east, and so on—look at the *situation of the features, and look for any correlation of human features with *relief features, such as *uplands, river valleys, or *coastal plains.

diurnal Within a day. The **diurnal temperature range** is the difference between the highest and lowest temperatures experienced over the 24-hour period.

diversification The production of a wider range of goods. In *agriculture, this means a move away from *monoculture, with all its dangers. For both *agriculture, and *industry, diversification lessens the risk of *over-reliance on one product.

domestic In economics, within a state, as in **domestic industry**, or **domestic trade**.

domesticated Tamed, and put to human use.

dormitory town A settlement largely made up of *commuters, who work elsewhere. Dormitory towns have relatively few shops and *services, since many people shop near their work, and some **dormitory villages** have no shops at all. The number of dormitory towns in the UK has increased in the past 30 years as a result of *counter-urbanization.

downstream Further down a river, towards its *mouth.

drain A channel cut in a wet site to take away the excess water. Rivers may be said to **drain** the land they flow over.

drainage 1. The natural pattern of streams, rivers, and lakes in an area. 2. The removal of excess water from the land by means of *drains.

drainage basin The area of land drained by a river and its *tributaries. It may also be called a river basin, or *catchment area. The edge of the drainage basin is the *watershed.

drift Material which has been removed by *glaciation and deposited somewhere else.

drift mine A mine where the seams are reached by a gently sloping underground road, rather than by a vertical shaft.

drought A long, continuous period of dry weather. In the UK, a drought is defined as 15 days with less than 0.2 mm of rain.

drowned coastline A coastline which has been flooded, either because the land has sunk or because the sea-level has risen (both are causes of **drowning**). A drowned valley can become a *ria or a *fiord.

drumlin A long, low hill, egg-shaped on a map, and made of *till; a feature of *glacial deposition.

dry farming Farming in *arid areas, which takes place without *irrigation. Water is saved by using such techniques as mulching, the use of *diguettes, *compost pits and *rock dams, frequent *fallowing, and working the soil to a very fine texture.

dry-point settlement A settlement on a somewhat higher site in a marshy, damp, or frequently flooded area.

dry valley A valley which has no permanent river, usually in a chalk or limestone area. The valley may have been cut during the *ice ages, when these rocks, which are both normally *permeable, were frozen. ▷▷escarpment.

DTM See *demographic transition model.

dual economy An economy made up of two very different systems—the *formal sector where the employee pays taxes and is 'officially' employed; and the *informal sector, where the worker is not registered with the tax authorities and has no sort of labour rights, or regular hours. Dual economies are found in many *developing countries where an *advanced economy exists side-by-side with a traditional economy, and the two have very little contact with each other.

dune A hill of sand. ▷ sand-dune, barchan, seif.

dust bowl An area of farmland which has been so *over-cropped or *overgrazed that severe *soil erosion has set in. The most famous dust bowl was created in Oklahoma, USA, in the 1930s. Dust storms were so frequent that many farmhouses were buried, thousands of tonnes of *topsoil were lost, and thousands of families had to leave the land, financially ruined.

dyke **1.** A *drainage channel. **2.** A vertical, or near-vertical sheet of *igneous rock which cuts across the *bedding planes of a rock. It is an *intrusion, formed when *magma forced its way through the rock strata, and then solidified. ▷▷ intrusion. **3.** A man-made bank, built alongside a river to reduce the risk of flooding.

E

earth pillar An upright column of soil that has been sheltered from erosion by a natural cap of stone on the top.

earthquake A sudden and violent movement, or *faulting, within the earth, followed by a series of jolts. Most earthquakes occur near *destructive plate margins; the San Francisco earthquake of 1906 occurred because of movement along the boundary of the North American and Pacific *plates. In that case, as in many earthquakes, most of the loss of life took place in the fires that broke out after the earthquake. The most commonly used scale to measure the intensity of an earthquake is the *Richter scale.

easting The reference lines which run North–South on a map, so-called because their numbers increase towards the East. They are the basis of the first half of a *grid reference.

EC *European Community.

ecology The study of plants and animals, including man, in the way that they are linked to each other and to their *habitats. A knowledge of the ecology of an area is vital for planners when they are considering the likely consequences of any change to the *environment.

economic Concerned with money; how it is earned and spent, and how it moves around. **Economic activity** is activity designed to increase wealth.

economically advanced country, economically developed country Two alternative terms for a *more developed country.

economic migrant Someone who *migrates in order to gain a better standard of living. ▷ political asylum, pull factor.

economy **1.** A saving. **Economies of scale** are the savings made by *mass production; up to a certain point, as the number of articles rises, the cost of each article falls. This occurs because the high *capital cost of machinery and buildings can be spread over a large number of goods. **2.** All the *economic activities of a nation—thus geographers refer to *less developed economies, *advanced economies, and so on.

ecosystem A community of plants and animals within a particular *environment; thus, we can talk about a desert ecosystem or an urban ecosystem. Ecosystems range in size from the whole earth to a drop of water. ▷ fragile ecosystem.

ED *enumeration district.

edaphic Of the soil.

edge A link (routeway) on a *topological map.

EEC European Economic Community, now **EC**. *European Community.

effluent Sewage, fertilizers in solution, or liquid industrial waste, as they flow into a river, stream, or lake.

EIA *environment.

electronics In geography, those industries making *high-technology goods, such as computers and calculators, based on the use of silicon chips. Since only small amounts of *raw materials are used, and since the products are valuable for their weight, electronics manufacturers need not locate near raw materials or *markets. They are often found in *science parks.

emigration The permanent movement of people *outward* from a state; an **emigrant** is the person who leaves a country for another (compare immigration, immigrant). ▷ economic migrant, migration, pull factor, push factor.

employment structure The make-up of a work-force. A simple breakdown looks at the percentages of workers in *primary (extractive), *secondary (manufacturing), *tertiary (service), and *quaternary (information) industry. As a country *develops, the percentage of workers in primary industry falls, and the percentages in secondary and tertiary industries, and possibly quaternary industry, rise.

energy The force needed to do work. Nearly all the forms of energy we use—*fossil fuels, wood, solar, wind, wave, and water power—come from the sun. Energy resources can be *renewable: winds, waves, and water; or *non-renewable: *fossil fuels such as coal, gas, and oil. The *development process increases demands for energy; on average, per capita energy use in more developed countries is twenty-five times greater than in less developed countries. The world demand for energy has increased so much that we have a potential shortage, which has been called an **energy crisis**.

enterprise zone In Britain, a *depressed or *derelict area which is to be revived by government action to lift normal *planning restrictions and taxation regulations. The Isle of Dogs, in London's East End, was one of the first enterprise zones.

enumeration district (ED) A unit of area used by *census-takers.

environment The surroundings. The **natural environment** includes the land, sea, and air; the **urban environment** is the city. Increasingly, any plan to change the environment must be examined to see how much it will affect the natural environment; this is **environmental impact assessment (EIA)**. **Environmental perception** is the impression you have of the environment; an Australian aborigine and a European, for example, would see the desert with very different eyes.

environmental restoration Attempting to re-create an environment after it has been altered or damaged by man; one example is *landscaping after *opencast mining. A more complex example is the attempt by the Norfolk Broads Authority to remove phosphorus and nitrate from Cockshoot Broad to reverse the effects of *eutrophication. This costly process involved pumping out thousands of tonnes of mud, and has only been partly successful.

equator The imaginary line, 40 076 km long, which runs east–west across the widest part of the earth, and divides the earth into the Northern and Southern *Hemispheres. Areas within 10° north and south of the equator are sometimes called **equatorial**.

equinox A time when the day and the night are the same length. In Britain, this happens on 21 March and 21 December .

ERDF *European Regional Development Fund.

erosion The wearing away of part of the land surface by the action of wind, water, ice, or gravity. These **erosive forces** can only transport material if it has first been broken up by *weathering. ▷ abrasion, attrition, corrasion, cycle of erosion, denudation, glacial erosion, hydraulic action, marine erosion, river erosion, mass movement, mud flow, plucking, quarrying, rock creep, saltation, slip, soil creep, solifluction.

erratic A large boulder of a different rock type from that of the area it is found in. Erratics found in East Anglia, for example, came originally from southern Norway. They are thought to have been carried to their new location by *glaciers and *ice sheets.

eruption *volcanic eruption.

escarpment A long, more or less uninterrupted, *ridge of high ground, often with a *scarp and a *dip slope. **Chalk escarpments** (or **chalk scarps**) are found in southern England; the South Downs are an example. ▷cuesta.

esker A low ridge of sands and gravels, 3 to 30 m high, winding across a lowland for distances from 10 m to 30 km. The ridge is formed of material deposited by streams of glacial *meltwater which ran under the ice. Examples are found in Finland and New England.

estuary The seaward part of a river mouth which is affected by the daily *tides, so that there is a mixture of fresh and salt water. Estuaries make good sites for fishing, for ports, and for *industrial development, since they provide flat land and deep water. Thames-side and Merseyside are examples. **Estuarine** means within an estuary.

ethnic Coming from a specific racial or language group. **Ethnic minorities** are people of a particular ethnic group who are outnumbered by the rest of the population. They are part of that state because of *immigration, and may suffer from discrimination. In some cases, such as South Africa, it is the ethnic minority—white Afrikaners—who hold power.

European Community (EC) First known as the **European Economic Community**, this is a *free-trading area made up (1993) of Belgium, The Netherlands, Luxemburg, France, Germany, Italy, United Kingdom, Denmark, Eire, Spain, Portugal, and Greece. The community was first set up to make *trade easier, but is now working towards greater co-operation in many other areas, such as employment, environment, and educational opportunities. ▷ Single European Market.

eutrophication The increase in plant nutrients dissolved in lakes and rivers as detergents, sewage, and fertilizers, washed from fields, pour into them. Frequently, the result is a massive increase in the growth of *algae, which block

the light from other pond plants which then cannot
*photosynthesize. This reduces the available oxygen in the
water, so that many animal forms of water life cannot survive. See also nitrate pollution.

evaporation The alteration, usually through heating, of
a liquid into a solid; liquid water **evaporates** to form
*water vapour. In this way, water vapour enters the
*atmosphere. ▷ water cycle.

evapotranspiration The release of water from the soil to
the *atmosphere by the processes of *evaporation and
plant *transpiration.

evergreen A plant which keeps most of its leaves
throughout the year. Most evergreens are *softwoods.
Compare *deciduous.

exfoliation A *weathering process where the outer layers
of a rock split off in sheets, or scales. It happens in deserts,
where days as hot as 40 ˚C are followed by nights as cold as
−10 ˚C. The strains set up in the rock as it expands and con-
tracts with this repeated heating and cooling finally cause
outer layers of the rock to split and fall away. Exfoliation
does not generally occur without some wetting of the
rock.

exhausted In geography, used up; the iron ores of South
Wales, for example, are now exhausted.

exotic Referring to a plant or animal not naturally occurring in a region, but having been *introduced* there by man.
In Britain, rhododendrons and mink are both exotic.

expanded town An already existing town, such as Bas-
ingstoke, which has been made larger, through the efforts
of city councils, to take overspill population from the
cramped and run-down *inner cities. Expanding a town is
cheaper than building a *new town, but there are no more
plans to expand towns in the UK.

Exponential growth

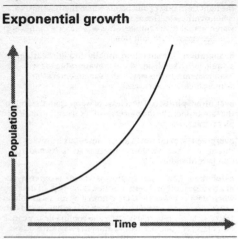

exponential growth

exponential growth One common example of exponential growth is growth which sees a doubling of numbers with every increase, such as 2, 4, 8, 16. *Malthus believed that population would grow in this way, and people still speak of **exponential population growth**.

exports *Goods and services sold by one country to another. Many Third World countries depend on the sale of **export crops**: cocoa from Ghana, coffee from Uganda, pineapples from Côte d'Ivoire are examples. This has caused problems, since the *real price of export crops has mostly fallen over the past fifteen years or so.

exposed coalfield A coalfield where the seams are at or near the surface. Exposed coalfields are easier to mine than *concealed ones, so that many exposed coalfields are now worked out. ▷ opencast mining.

extensive In geography, using a low level of *inputs. **Extensive agriculture** has relatively small inputs of *capital and labour, and yields per hectare are modest; an intensively farmed area of East Anglia might give six times the wheat yield of an **extensively farmed** Canadian prairie holding. Other examples of extensively farmed areas range from sheep farming in the Australian outback to *nomadic pastoralism. ▷ von Thunen model.

extraction In geography, the removal of a *raw material from where it is found. **Extractive industries**, such as *mining or *lumbering, take out raw materials. They are also called *primary industries.

extreme Far from the average. An **extreme climate**, such as that of the Canadian prairies has a very wide annual *temperature range. Compare with *temperate climate.

F

facility In geography, the means or equipment to do something, such as port, or cargo-handling facilities.

factor Anything that, partly or entirely, influences an outcome. In geography it is usual to speak of **physical factors**, such as *climate, *relief, *soils and *vegetation, and **human factors**, such as history, politics, *culture, or the *economy.

factory farming The very *intensive rearing and use of animals such as veal calves or battery hens. The animals are often kept indoors, in very cramped conditions, and growth hormones are often used to increase yields.

fallow Land which is not farmed. In the *bush-fallowing system, the land is left to recover its fertility; in Europe, many farmers are encouraged to leave their land fallow to solve problems of over-production. ▷ set-aside, rotation.

false colour In a satellite picture, a colour given to an image picked up by the scanner on a wavelength, such as infra-red, that we cannot see. A picture using false colours is a **false colour image**.

family planning *birth control.

famine A very serious shortage of food, leading to the deaths of a large number of people over a wide area. Today, the most common causes of famine are drought and civil war. Famines differ from constant hunger in that they occur only infrequently and affect a limited number of people, who usually die directly of starvation. *Hunger is possibly a more serious problem than famine in the world today. ▷ malnutrition.

farm fragmentation The division of a farm into small, scattered units. This may occur if a farm is divided between the children on the death of the farmer, and it may also take place in areas where *bush-fallowing was practised. A **fragmented farm** is inefficient to run, and many governments have tried to solve this problem by *land reform.

farming Growing crops and/or raising animals. ▷ arable farming, contract farming, dry farming, extensive farming, hill farming, intensive farming, mixed farming, pastoral farming.

fault A split in the earth's crust, along which rocks on either or both sides have slipped. The formation of these cracks is known as **faulting**, and it happens after pressure has built up within the crust. In a **normal fault**, rocks move down the slope of the fault; in a **reverse fault** they move up the slope. In a **transcurrent fault**, the movement is horizontal; this is the case along the San Andreas fault in California. Earthquakes result from movement along a fault, and **faulted** areas, being lines of weakness, are often more easily *eroded than **non-faulted** zones; **fault-guided valleys** are common. ✍

favela In Brazil, a *shanty town.

feedback loop An event, or series of events, in a chain of circumstances which serve to bring about a repeat of the initial event. This *cycle of poverty is an example of a feedback loop:

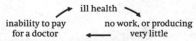

ill health

inability to pay   no work, or producing
for a doctor   very little

federation A system of government where several states are united for some policies—like defence—but are independent for others, such as education. This is the **federal** system, found, for example, in Germany and the USA.

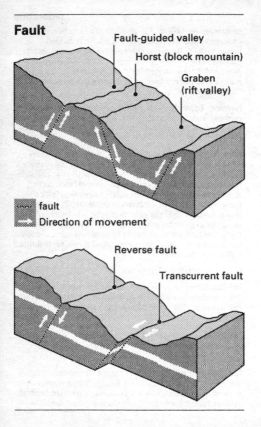

Fault

Fault-guided valley

Horst (block mountain)

Graben (rift valley)

::::: fault

Direction of movement

Reverse fault

Transcurrent fault

Field sketch

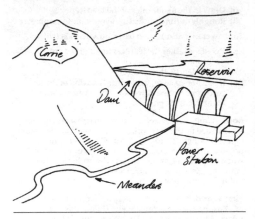

fell A rocky upland of moorland or *rough grazing. Fells are often *common land.

fen A wet, *peaty lowland, especially in East Anglia.

fertilizer Any substance added to the soil which increases its fertility, and thus improves yields. *Organic fertilizers are naturally occurring substances, such as manure, fishmeal, or compost, while *inorganic fertilizers are man-made. Most contain at least one compound of potassium, phosphorus, or nitrogen. When excess fertilizer is washed from the fields and into streams, *eutrophication may take place. Because of this, the use of *leguminous plants, which take nitrogen from the air and fix it in the soil may be preferable to the use of fertilizers.

field sketch A field sketch highlights certain features, but is not meant to be a work of art. To draw a field sketch:

(i) Draw in the major lines of the landscape.
(ii) Roughly outline the features you want to emphasize.

To answer a GCSE question based on a field sketch:

(i) Decide whether the features highlighted are *physical or *human.
(ii) Try to identify the features.
(iii) If you are asked to, look at the *location of the features, or describe how they were formed, correctly identifying the *processes* involved. ✍

fiord A long, deep, steep-sided, and narrow arm of the sea, formed by the *'drowning' of a glacially eroded valley (*glacial trough). Fiords tend to be shallower at the *mouth because the glacier had less power to erode at the point when it spread out from the glaciated valley into the lowlands. Fiords may be found in Scotland, Norway, British Columbia, and New Zealand. ✍

First World Before the break-up of communism in Eastern Europe and the former Soviet Union, this term referred to the *West. The First World could also be described as the capitalist world. ▷Third World.

fishing A *primary industry, operating most successfully on the *continental shelves, and currently, in the *EC, in difficulties because of over-fishing. **Fish farms** are man-made fisheries, using artificial or natural lakes. The fish can be moved from one pond to another as they grow, and their diet can be carefully checked.

fjord See *fiord.

flash flood A sudden and very violent flood, usually in a *semi-arid area, often caused by a rare burst of very heavy rain. Because they occur in generally dry areas, they are very difficult to predict, and can be extremely destructive.

flood An overflow of water, from a river, or from the sea, on to the land. The rise of a river during a time of flooding can be charted on a **flood hydrograph**, which shows the increase (and later the decrease) in *discharge over time. The **flood event** stands out clearly from the normal base flow. ▷ hydrograph.

Basic **flood prevention** methods include deepening the river, digging extra, overflow, channels, building dams and *levees, and planting trees on the hill slopes above the river (▷ afforestation). Sometimes settlements in areas of **flood risk** have been rebuilt on higher ground.

floodplain The relatively flat land stretching from either bank of a river to the bottom of the valley slopes, cut both

Fiord

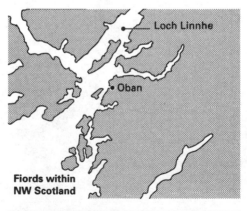

Loch Linnhe

• Oban

Fiords within NW Scotland

Flow line

Major migrations to Birmingham, 1965

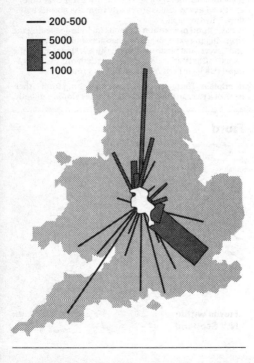

by the river and by the migration of its *meanders. Since floodplains are made of fertile *alluvium, they are usually good farming areas. ▷▷ river features.

flow line A diagram showing movements, for example, of goods, people, services, or information, across a map. The thickness of the lines of movement varies with the size of the movements. To draw a flow line graph:

(i) Pencil in the lines of movement on the base map.
(ii) Choose a suitable scale of widths; large enough to show the variations but not so large that the map is almost all blacked out. If you have a very wide range of values, you can class together all the lowest values (for example, below 100, as in the illustration) and show them as a single line.
(iii) Remember that when two lines meet and become one, their thickness must be equal to the width of both.   ✍

fluvial To do with rivers.

fluvio-glacial Related to *meltwater from glaciers. *Kames, *eskers, and *outwash plains, are all **fluvio-glacial features**.   ✍

focus The location of the source of an *earthquake.

fodder crop A crop grown for animal feed. Some fodder crops, such as hay, are fed directly to the animals; others are processed into foods like *silage, or cattle-cake.

fog A cloud of water droplets which are suspended in the air and which cut down visibility to less than 1000 m. Fog occurs when the *water vapour in the air is cooled to *dew point. This cooling can occur when the air is in contact with cold ground—a common cause of fogs in autumn— this is **radiation fog**; or when it passes over cold sea currents—**advection fog**.   ✍

Fluvio-glacial features

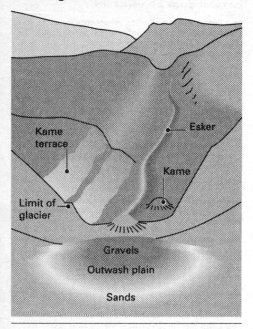

Kame terrace

Esker

Kame

Limit of glacier

Gravels

Outwash plain

Sands

föhn, foehn A dry, warm and gusty wind, blowing down from a mountain range. It gets warmer as it blows downslope because it is under greater and greater air pressure.

Radiation fog

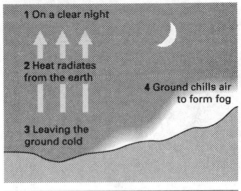

1 On a clear night

2 Heat radiates from the earth

4 Ground chills air to form fog

3 Leaving the ground cold

The common name for a föhn wind in Canada is the 'chinook'. When the chinook blows, temperatures rise rapidly, and it is said to have a bad effect on people's health, and even on their mental stability!

fold Buckled or bent rock *strata. **Folding** is caused by earth movements, such as the movement of *plates. An upfold is an anticline; a downfold a syncline, and some folds are broken, or fractured:

fold mountains have been formed by very large-scale, complicated folding, often caused by the movement of *plates. The Alps are examples of **young fold mountains** (65 million years *BP); the Scottish Highlands are **old fold mountains** (395 million years *BP), but the latter are now very much worn down by *erosion.

Fold mountains

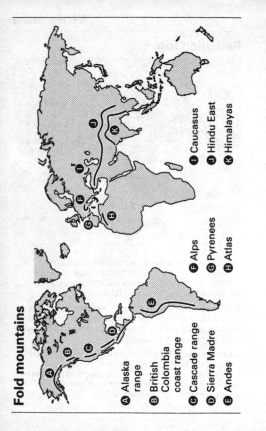

- Ⓐ Alaska range
- Ⓑ British Colombia coast range
- Ⓒ Cascade range
- Ⓓ Sierra Madre
- Ⓔ Andes
- Ⓕ Alps
- Ⓖ Pyrenees
- Ⓗ Atlas
- Ⓘ Caucasus
- Ⓙ Hindu East
- Ⓚ Himalayas

Food chain

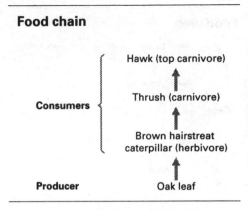

Consumers {

Hawk (top carnivore)

↑

Thrush (carnivore)

↑

Brown hairstreat
caterpillar (herbivore)

↑

Producer   Oak leaf

---

food chain A series of feeding relationships between living things, starting with the producers—the green plants which create new food, using the sun's energy—leading to *herbivores and *carnivores.

In real life, things are not so simple, and the feeding relationships between organisms are more accurately shown in a **food web**.

foot A unit of measurement, roughly equal to 30 cm.

footloose Not tied to any particular place. **Footloose industries**, like publishing or electronics, do not use much *raw material, and produce goods of relatively high value for their weight, so they have more choice in their location than *heavy industries.

forest A large area of woodland, either natural, or planted by man. **Forestry** is the management and use of forests and forest products (compare *lumbering),

Food web

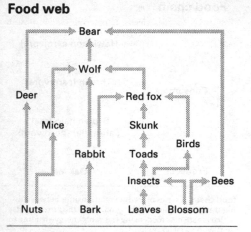

and **sustainable forestry** includes replanting as well as felling trees so that the resource is renewed. ▷ renewable resources.

form Shape. The word is often used for the shape of towns and cities, which is better described as **urban form**.

formal When used in the setting of employment, this describes a job where the employee pays taxes and is 'officially' employed; thus it is usual to refer to **formal employment**, and people with this sort of job are said to work in the **formal sector**. ▷ informal sector.

formal region A region with very similar features throughout, such as Amazonia, or the Mediterranean

lands. Geographers used to call these 'natural regions'.
Compare *functional region.

fossil fuel Any fuel which is found underground, buried
within *sedimentary rock, and made from the remains of
plants and/or animals. The most important are oil, natural
gas, coal, brown coal, and peat, all of which are *non-
renewable resources. Burning fossil fuels can cause *pollution and *acid rain. For these reasons, many governments
are concerned to develop *renewable energy resources.

fragile ecosystem An *ecosystem which is easily, and
often incurably, altered by man. The *tropical rain forest is
a particularly fragile ecosystem.

fragmentation *farm fragmentation.

free port A port, or an area within a port, where goods
passing through are not subject to customs duties. This
means that manufacturers can process imported raw
materials and then export them without being charged
import taxes. Free ports, like Singapore and Copenhagen
are thus attractive sites for *manufacturing industry.

free trade zone An area within a country where goods
are not subject to customs duties; thus having the same
advantages to a manufacturer as does a *free port. In addition, many free trade zones do not uphold strict safety
conditions for their factory workers, and do not allow
trade union activity, so that they can sack workers who
might want higher wages or maternity leave. For these
reasons, many *Third World workers see the establish-
ment of free trade zones in their countries as a mixed
blessing.

freeze–thaw The *weathering of rock which happens
when water seeps into cracks in a rock (1), and then
freezes. When water freezes, it expands (2), and the force
of this expansion widens the cracks and breaks up the
rock (3). For freeze–thaw to be most effective, tempera-

Freeze-thaw

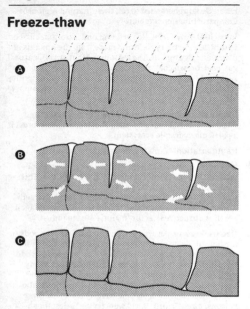

tures should fluctuate around freezing point. Rocks which have been exposed to freeze–thaw often break up to form *scree.

freight Anything which is transported. ▷ air freight.

friction of distance Another term for *distance decay.

front The border zone between two contrasting types of *air mass. The air masses may be different in temperature, or humidity, or both. A **warm front** marks the beginning of the *warm sector—the warm air at the centre of a *depression—and a **cold front** the beginning of the cold air at the back of a depression. Most fronts bring **frontal rain**; in Britain, a warm front usually gives about five hours of constant wet weather while a cold front brings heavier, but shorter-lasting, rain.

frontier The *boundary between one *state and another. With the introduction of the Single Market in the *European Community, and within the Community, the impact of frontiers on migration and customs duties has become much less.

frost Frozen *dew, or frozen *fog, forming at or near ground level. On still, clear nights, heavier, cold air can flow down from the hill-tops to collect in depressions or steep-sided valleys to form **frost hollows**.

frost-shattering Another term for *freeze–thaw.

FTZ *free trade zone.

fuel Any source of energy. ▷energy, fossil fuel, renewable resource, non-renewable resource. *Less developed countries tend to depend heavily on **fuelwood**; this has led to *deforestation, and subsequent *soil erosion.

function Purpose, or use. The functions of a *central place include the provision of *goods and *services, and the total number of its functions are said to increase with its size. ▷central place theory.

functional classification Classifying something according to its *function. A **functional classification of cities** could include categories like administration, defence, tourism. A **functional region** is a region marked out by its function, such as a drainage basin or a Health Authority area.

G

gale A strong wind. ▷ Beaufort scale.

gallon 8 pints, or about 4·5 litres.

garden city A settlement planned to combine the advantages of living in a town without the crowded squalid conditions of Victorian cities. The first Garden City was Letchworth, built in 1903. Housing *densities were low, roads broad, and parks, open spaces, and allotments were plentiful. Similarly, a **garden suburb** is a planned *suburban development with open spaces and low-density housing. Hampstead Garden Suburb was built in 1907.

GATT *General Agreement on Tariffs and Trade.

GDP * gross domestic product.

General Agreement on Tariffs and Trade (GATT) An agreement between the states of the free world to encourage the removal of *trade barriers, such as *quotas and customs duties, in order to encourage international trade. If GATT breaks down, damaging *trade wars could follow.

general circulation of the atmosphere The world-scale system of winds and pressure belts which return seasonally or persist throughout the year. The winds transport heat from the *equator to the poles, and are driven by the powerful differences in the heat received by the sun at different parts of the earth's surface (*insolation). They blow diagonally as a result of the rotation of the earth.

gentrification The renovation of run-down *inner-city areas as wealthier, middle class buyers move in, attracted by relatively cheap housing, and by nearness to the city centres. The original residents gradually move out, often

General circulation of the atmosphere

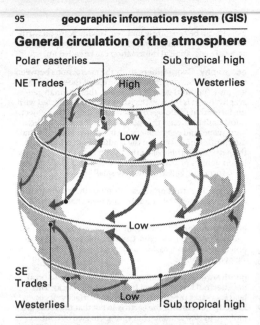

Polar easterlies

Sub tropical high

NE Trades

High

Westerlies

Low

Low

SE Trades

Westerlies

Low

Sub tropical high

as their leases fall in, but sometimes after harassment
from landlords who are keen to sell to the incomers at
higher prices. Many local authorities encourage
gentrification by granting mortgages to newcomers, as
this process can form a part of *urban renewal.

geographic information system (GIS) A store of geographical data kept, in digital form, on a computer. GISs
can be linked directly to remote sensors, so that the infor-

mation can be constantly updated. For any point on earth locatable (identifiable) by the use of coordinates, a vast array of geographical information can be called up.

geography Geographers study the interactions between man and the *environment. At one end of the spectrum lies pure *physical geography; at the other, *human geography, but it is the way that the former is connected with the latter that could be considered the core of the subject. Another definition is that geography is the study of the *landscape, and geographers are interested in the *spatial distribution of features in the landscape—in other words the *pattern of distribution* of the feature, whether it be population density or annual rainfall—and this can be on any scale from the *global to the very small.

geology The study of the earth's rocks: their formation and development, their nature and their characteristic *landforms.

geomorphology The study of *landforms: how they look and how they were formed. **Geomorphic processes** are processes such as *erosion or *deposition which have shaped landforms.

geothermal energy Energy gathered from the natural **geothermal heat** released from the earth's rocks. This heat increases the deeper beneath the surface you go; indeed, the centre of the earth is so hot that the rocks are molten. In New Zealand, hot springs, heated by contact with hot, underground rocks, are used as a source of heating. In other areas, water is forced down through boreholes, heated as it meets hot rock, and then pumped to the surface. This process has been used successfully as a source of heating in Southampton.

gerrymandering Redrawing constituency boundaries in order to gain a political advantage. One way is to concentrate most of the opposition's vote into a few electoral districts so that major support for them actually results in only a few successful candidates.

ghetto A part of a city, often but not always a slum area, occupied by a minority group. The word was first used in Europe, from the Middle Ages, for the areas Jews were *forced* to live in, but it has now spread to include other groups in 'unofficial' ghettos, particularly blacks in the USA. Life within the ghetto is distinctly different from life outside it, and the prejudices of the majority outside tend to keep the minority inside the ghetto.

Gini coefficient

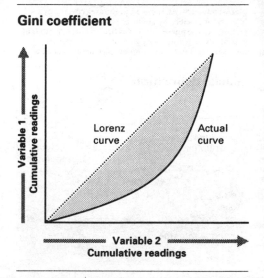

Gini coefficient In a Lorenz curve, a measurement of the difference between the actual distribution of some variable, like population or income, and a perfectly even distribution. This coefficient is calculated by dividing the area between the diagonal (shaded in the diagram) and the Lorenz curve, by the *total* area beneath the diagonal. The lower the Gini coefficient, the more evenly spread the variable.   ✍

GIS *geographic information system.

glacial Having to do with a *glacier.

glacial advance An increase in the area covered by a *glacier, or glaciers. Most present-day glaciers advance in winter, but the phases known as *ice ages were periods of glacial advance over a very wide area. Correspondingly, most glaciers retreat in summer. Each ice age ended with

Glacial deposition

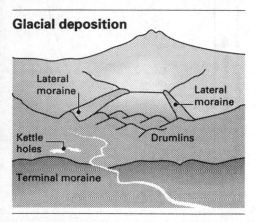

a major period of **glacial retreat**. Both advance and retreat are caused by changes in the *climate. ▷ climatic change.

glacial deposition The laying down of *sediments which have been removed and transported by a *glacier. The sediments—known as *till, or *drift*—are deposited when the ice melts. Features of glacial deposition include *drumlins, *erratics, *kettle holes, and many types of *moraine. ▷ fluvio-glacial. ✍

glacial erosion The wearing away and removal of rocks and soil by glacier ice. Ice is not particularly strong, and glacial erosion works best on rocks which have already been weakened by *freeze–thaw, jointing, or cracking. Two major processes are *quarrying (plucking), and *abrasion. Over time, glacial erosion can produce such spectacular features as *corries, *artes, *pyramidal peaks, *glacial troughs, *hanging valleys, and *truncated spurs, together with smaller-scale features like *roches moutonnées. ✍

glacial trough A flat-floored, steep-sided valley, shaped by *glacial erosion. Above the trough are the high-level tributaries known as *hanging valleys, and the flat floors are often occupied by lakes or areas of *moraine. Any *spurs which once jutted out into the valley will now be *truncated. ▷▷ glacial erosion.

glaciation The effect of a glacier on a landscape. Usually, an area is said to have been **glaciated** when it has been altered by *glacial erosion, rather than by *glacial deposition, but either could be implied.

glacier A slow-moving 'river' of ice, fed at its source by snow fall. Glaciers move at about 1 m a day, although the rate varies with the temperature of the icy base, and great cracks called *crevasses open and close in the ice as it moves. ▷ glacial advance, glacial deposition, glacial erosion, glacial trough, glaciation. ✍

gley soils Soils with mottled grey and yellow patches caused by repeated *waterlogging.

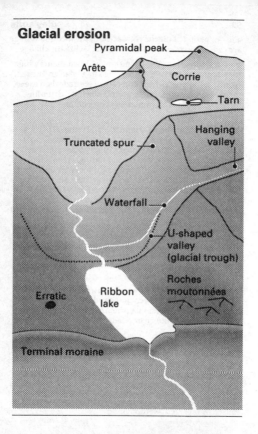

Glacial erosion

Pyramidal peak

Arête

Corrie

Tarn

Hanging valley

Truncated spur

Waterfall

U-shaped valley (glacial trough)

Roches moutonnées

Erratic

Ribbon lake

Terminal moraine

Glacier

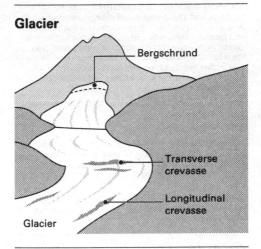

Bergschrund

Transverse
crevasse

Longitudinal
crevasse

Glacier

global warming, greenhouse effect The warming of the
earth's atmosphere. Man's activities have caused increasingly large amounts of *greenhouse gases like *carbon
monoxide, methane, chlorofluorocarbons, and *water
vapour to enter the air. These gases are all very effective at
absorbing the heat which radiates out from the earth; as a
result, it is claimed that average temperatures in the
atmosphere are rising, and will continue to rise unless
emissions of greenhouse gases are cut. The consequences
could be very serious. If the polar *ice-sheets' caps begin to
melt more rapidly, sea-levels will rise, and many low-lying
areas will be swamped, with a loss of vital farming, hous-

ing, retail, commercial, and industrial areas. Habitats would be lost. The climate could change; some scientists predict the expansion of deserts, others think that storms will increase. Those who believe that global warming is taking place agree that emissions of greenhouse gases must be cut. This could be achieved by burning less *fossil fuel (either by using fossil fuel more efficiently, or by using *alternative fuels), by halting *deforestation, and by planting more trees.

globe A sphere, or a model of the earth. **Global**, however, means world-wide.

GNP *gross national product.

Gondwanaland A 'supercontinent', formed when *Pangaea split, and composed of what are now the *southern continents*: South America, Africa, Madagascar, Antarctica, Australasia, and India. ▷▷ continental drift, plate tectonics.

good Any object which can be bought, sold, given, received, or exchanged. ▷ high-order good, low-order good, range of a good.

Graded profile

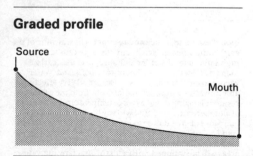

Source

Mouth

gorge A narrow, steep-sided river valley, specifically in a region of *karst. Cheddar Gorge, in Somerset, is a classic example. ▷▷ karst scenery.

graben Another name for a *rift valley.

graded profile The long profile of a river as it would be if all the sudden *breaks of slope—as, for example, at a water-fall—were eroded away. In theory, if a river were left to erode without any disturbance, it would finally achieve a graded profile.

gradient 1. A measurement of the steepness of a slope. The average gradient between two points, as in the figure below, can be calculated as:

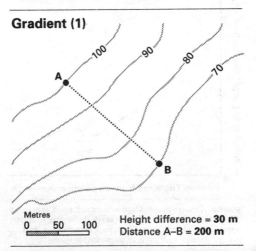

Gradient (1)

Metres
0   50   100

Height difference = **30 m**
Distance A–B = **200 m**

$$\frac{\text{difference in height between points}}{\text{distance between points}} \times 100$$

that is, $\dfrac{30 \times 100}{200} = 15\%$

2. A measurement of change in certain aspects of human geography such as the density of population. The graph in the figure below shows the population density gradient in a town.

Gradient (2)

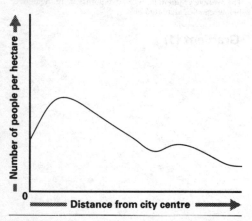

granite A coarse-grained *igneous rock, formed as magma forced its way up to, but did not reach the surface (▷ intrusion). Granite forms moorlands, such as Dartmoor, *tors, and spectacular cliffs. It is an important building material, and *weathers to form china clay, used in pottery-making.

grass strip A strip of grass, several metres wide, running along a contour, planted to cut the speed of water flowing down a slope and thus designed to stop *soil erosion.

gravel pit A quarry for the extraction of the naturally occurring, rounded rock fragments known as **gravel**.

gravity model A *model of the attraction of two central places. The amount of movement—such as *migration, or *commuting—between the two places is said to be an expression of the size of the settlements and the distance between them:

$$\text{Amount of movement} = \frac{\text{population of town A} \times \text{population of town B}}{\text{distance between towns}}$$

The model has been used by planners to predict traffic flows.

grazing Putting animals out to eat grass. ▷ rough grazing.

great circle Any circle drawn around the earth whose centre is the same as the centre of the earth. **Great circle routes** are routes, usually flown by aircraft, that use part of a great circle, and they are always the shortest distance between two points on the earth's surface. The *equator is the only line of *latitude which is also a great circle.

green belt An area of land, usually around a town or city, where new building is rarely permitted. Green belts were created in order to cut down *urban sprawl, and to keep the countryside within reach of town-dwellers.

greenfield site An area of countryside which can be used for new development. Greenfield sites do not need demolition work, and are often in pleasant surroundings, so they are attractive to developers. Many *footloose industries are

on greenfield sites at the edge of towns and cities and near
*motorways.

greenhouse effect Another term for *global warming.

greenhouse gas Any gas, such as *carbon dioxide,
methane, *ozone, or *water vapour, which contributes to
*global warming (the greenhouse effect).

green manure A *leguminous crop, such as clover, which
will extract nitrogen from the air, and fix it in the soil,
thus improving soil fertility without the use of chemical
fertilizers. ▷ organic farming.

green revolution A huge increase in *arable output,
brought about by a package of high-yielding, and often
fast-growing crops (*high-yielding varieties), together with
the fertilizers, herbicides, and irrigation needed to make
them grow. The green revolution has succeeded in that
output has risen, and some countries, like the Philippines,
have changed from being food importers to food export-
ers. However, the package was only of benefit to those who
could afford it. In some cases, landlords raised rents, or
evicted peasants from the land once they saw how much
more their land could produce with the green revolution
package. In addition, much of the increased production
was exported, so that the poor were often no less hungry,
and the gap between rich and poor has widened.

grid line A reference line on a map. Lines running
North–South are *eastings; lines running East–West are
*northings. The lines intersect to form **grid squares**, and
together they can be used to create a **grid reference**. To
quote a grid reference for a particular point, proceed as
follows:

1. From the illustration below, first give the grid reference for point X from the easting. The first two numbers
are the numbers of the easting to the left of X, that is, 68.
X is approximately five-tenths of a grid square beyond the
easting, so the third number of the reference is 5: so far
the reference is therefore 685.

Grid line

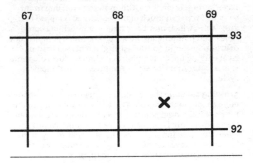

2. The second part of the reference uses the northing below point X, that is, 92. Since X is three-tenths of a grid square north of the grid line, the last number of the reference is 3, and the second part of the reference is therefore 923. The **six-figure grid reference** for X is therefore 685923. ✍️

gross domestic product (GDP) The total value of all the *goods and *services produced within a state in one year. This total includes production from people who reside in that state, but are not of that nationality. Geographers tend to use GDP and *GNP interchangeably, but there is a difference between the two statistics.

gross national product (GNP) The total value of all the *goods and *services produced by the *nationals of a state in one year, whether they were living in that state during the year, or not. Geographers tend to use GNP and *GDP interchangeably, but there is a difference between the two statistics.

groundwater Underground water, stored in the spaces within porous rock. The upper level of groundwater is the *water-table; where the water-table meets the ground surface, *springs often form. Groundwater is an important source of water in much of the world, and is tapped by digging wells, which may be *artesian, or by drilling boreholes, and pumping up the water. Too much pumping out of groundwater in South-East England has led to some rivers drying up, and tipping of pollutants down old mine shafts can contaminate this resource. ▷▷ hydrological cycle.

growing season The season when temperatures are high enough for plants to grow. This will vary according to the needs of individual plants, but very little will grow when the temperature is below 4 °C. Areas within a country where the growing season begins early, like Jersey in the UK, have an advantage because they can produce early crops, like new potatoes, for the market.

growth pole A point within a region where *economic growth is especially strong. Under the influence of the growth pole, the economy of the surrounding region may also improve, and it is this feature which has caused many planners to try to create growth poles in depressed regions. The French *metropoles d'équilibre* were towns specially selected for government in the hope that increased prosperity in these towns would spread into the surrounding region. ▷ core-periphery, cumulative causation.

groyne A breakwater, running seaward from the land, made to stop beach material being removed by *longshore drift. ▷▷ marine deposition.

gryke A joint in a block of limestone, which has been widened by the action of mildly acidic rainwater on the rock. ▷ karst.

gully A cutting made by flowing water which is usually steep-sided with a flattened floor.

H

habitat The area which is suitable for a plant or animal to live in, and where it has a good chance of survival. Habitats range in size from a puddle to the *savanna.

hachure The shading on a *relief map which helps to give an impression of the slope of the land.

hail A type of snow, consisting of a roughly spherical lump of ice, 5 mm or more in diameter. A **hailstone** forms when a frozen raindrop is caught in the strong draughts of upward-moving air found in *cumulo-nimbus clouds. Each time it is whirled upwards it attracts more ice, getting heavier and heavier until it finally falls to earth.

hamlet A small, *rural settlement without services or shops, and often without a church.

hanging valley A valley located so high above the major valley it runs into that there is a sharp drop between the two, caused because the main valley has been *glacially eroded much more severely than the *tributary valley. A waterfall often falls if there is a river running from the hanging valley into the larger valley. ▷▷ glacial erosion.

harbour A place of shelter where ships can tie up. **Natural harbours**, like San Francisco, are located in *bays which are often sheltered by hills or mountains; **man-made harbours**, like Tema, Ghana, need specially constructed *quays and *breakwaters to protect shipping from the weather, and are usually only developed along coasts where natural harbours are few.

hardwood A slow-growing, *deciduous tree, such as oak. **Tropical hardwoods** include mahogany and ebony, and can be very valuable, but, unlike *softwoods, do not grow in pure stands.

hazard See *natural hazard.

HDI *Human Development Index.

headland A point of higher land jutting out into the sea, often made of a resistant rock, such as *granite, and surviving because of *differential erosion. ▷▷ marine erosion.

heath A naturally occurring area of sandy lowland, covered with shrubs like heather and gorse. **Heathlands** tend to be left uncultivated because their soils are poor.

heat island A large built-up area where the air temperatures are warmer than those in the countryside around it. The extra heat is given off by central heating, vehicles and industry, and the difference in heat can be up to 5 °C.

heavy industry Any *manufacturing industry which needs large quantities of bulky *raw materials, such as iron and steel making, shipbuilding and chemical manufacturing. Heavy industries are often tied, that is, located near the source of their raw materials.

hectare 10 000 m^2, or 2.471 acres.

hemisphere Half a sphere; in geography, half of the world. It is common to hear of the **Northern and Southern Hemispheres**, but also possible to speak of the **Western** and **Eastern Hemispheres**.

HEP *hydroelectric power.

herbicide Weedkiller.

herbivore An animal that eats only plant material.

hierarchy Any way of kind of organization based on ranks or classes. Geographers put many features into hierarchies, such as rivers or shopping centres; a **settlement hierarchy** places cities, towns, and villages in order of size, or status. It is a characteristic of a hierarchy that there are fewer occurrences in the top ranks than there are in the lower ranks, but this does not always follow completely, as can be seen in the upper ranks of this UK settlement hierarchy, which is based on *size*.

settlement size	number of settlements
above 1 million	2
500 000–1 million	3
250 000–500 000	20
150 000–250 000	34
100 000–150 000	25
75 000–100 000	35
40 000–75 000	133
20 000–40 000	185
10 000–20 000	220

A hierarchy based on the *number of functions* in each settlement need not be the same as a hierarchy based on settlement size.

high A shorter term for an area of high *atmospheric pressure (anything over about 996 *mb); in other words, for an *anticyclone.

highland In the UK, land over about 200 m.

high order Describing a *good or *service which is only provided where there is a large enough potential market (*threshold population) to justify its supply. High order goods and services tend to be specialties which people do not often buy, such as expensive hi-fi equipment or investment advice, and they are thus located in large *central places, which may then be called **high order settlements**. High order settlements have a large *range and a large *catchment area, and *settlement hierarchies can be constructed, based on the numbers of high order functions.

high technology The use of complicated, sophisticated techniques, together with advanced, and often expensive, equipment. A **high technology approach** is a costly approach, so that high technology is not always *appropriate technology.

high-yielding varieties (HYVs) Crops which have been particularly bred to produce much heavier crops than the varieties traditionally grown. *Cereal HYVs have to have shorter, thicker stems to carry the weight of the extra grain: examples are Mexican Dwarf Wheat and 'Miracle Rice' (IR-8). Unfortunately, HYVs are expensive, do not produce seed for next year, need exactly the right *inputs of water, *fertilizer, *herbicides, and *insecticides, and can be distressingly prone to disease. ▷ green revolution.

hill farming Farming in *highland areas. In the UK, hill farming is carried out in uplands like the Pennines and the Lake District, and here, as elsewhere in the *EC, hill farming is relatively inefficient because conditions of *accessibility, slope, soils, and climate are not favourable. Hill farming is farming on *marginal land. Some farmers cover the increased costs by specializing; some supplement their income with tourism, but most are kept in business only because of EC *subsidies.

hinterland The area around a settlement which uses the *goods and *services found in that settlement; the area served by a settlement. ▷ catchment area, sphere of influence. Some geographers use the term only in connection with *ports. ▷ urban field.

histogram A type of *bar graph where the *data are sorted into groups, or classes, and the height of each bar indicates the numbers in each class. If the boundaries of the classes are changed, the histogram can look quite different. To construct a histogram:

(i) Decide on the number of classes you will use; at GCSE level, six is about the maximum. Class sizes can be regular, as in 0–10, 11–20, 21–30, and so on, but they

Histogram

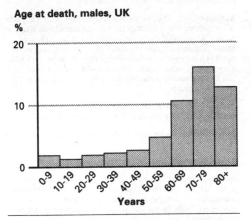

Age at death, males, UK

need not be. *Make sure the start of each class group is one unit higher than the end of the preceding group (as above).*
(ii) Sort the data into the relevant classes.
(iii) Count how many figures there are in each class.
(iv) Show the number of occurrences in each class as a bar graph.

hi-tech A term used to describe industries using the latest machinery and methods, and generally producing goods which are comparatively small in size, but quite costly, like computer games. Hi-tech industries are often located in *business parks or *science parks, and the areas of the UK known as silicon fen (Cambridgeshire) and silicon glen (Central Scotland) have important concentrations of hi-tech industry. Nevertheless, hi-tech industries are good examples of *footloose industries because goods are low in weight and high in value.

honeypot site The part of any tourist area which attracts most visitors. Since visitor numbers to attractions like some UK *National Parks are becoming unmanageable, many planners suggest that the favourite spots are developed as honeypot sites to cater for the majority, with good access roads, restaurants, toilets, and gift shops, leaving the less *accessible areas for the more energetic minority to enjoy in peace.

horizon A clearly distinguishable layer within the soil, usually detectable because of its colour and/or texture.

horn Another name for a *pyramidal peak. ▷▷ glacial erosion.

horst Another name for a *block mountain.

horticulture The growing of flowers, fruit, and vegetables. The most favoured spots for horticulture either have a mild, moist climate, or are located near big cities where demand is high. Horticulture is an example of *intensive agriculture.

hot spot A part of the earth's *crust which is thin enough to let *magma through to form a volcano. Most of the volcanoes which are not at *plate margins are at hot spots.

household The occupants of one unit of housing, whether it be a flat, maisonette, caravan, or house. **Household amenities** are the facilities available to the household, and these may include gas, electricity, central heating, lavatories, bathrooms, and hot and cold running water.

housing tenure The conditions under which a *household inhabits its home. Common systems of housing tenure include *owner-occupation and renting. ▷land tenure.

Hoyt model See sector model.

Human Development Index A measurement of people's well-being made by combining a number of indicators, such as *life expectancy and atmospheric *pollution. The index was devised by the United Nations, and, in 1993, showed that the quality of life was highest in Japan and lowest in Guinea.

human geography The study of the man-made *landscape; how it was formed, and how it appears, together with an investigation of the processes which shaped it.

humidity The amount of *water vapour held in the *atmosphere. **Relative humidity** is calculated using the following formula:

$$\frac{\text{amount of water vapour actually present in air}}{\text{maximum amount of water vapour}} \times 100$$
$$\text{which could be held in air}$$

hunger Incessant hunger kills more people than *famine does, usually because the severely undernourished have little resistance to disease. Every day, enough children to fill 240 jumbo jets die of hunger, even though enough food is produced to feed the entire world. ▷malnutrition, undernourishment.

hunting and gathering A simple form of feeding a society by hunting wild animals and collecting wild fruit and berries. There are very few **hunter-gatherers** left in today's world; a few groups remain in places like the Amazon basin or the Australian *bush, but their life-style is threatened by *development.

hurricane Also known as a **typhoon**, or **tropical storm**, a hurricane is an intense spinning storm, as much as 650 km across. Violent winds of 140 km/hr or more are accom-

Hurricane

Eye

panied by torrential rain. Hurricanes seem to be caused by
rising air, which is perhaps pulled up by disturbances in
the upper air. Moist air at ground level is pulled inwards
and upwards, and the spin is caused by the rotation of the
earth. As the air rises it cools, and water vapour condenses
out, releasing heat, which gives the hurricane more
energy. At the middle of the hurricane is a still centre
known as the *eye*. Hurricanes form in distinct belts north
and south of the equator, where temperatures are high
and the rotational effect of the earth is strong, and die out
when they move more than a few miles inland. They cause
immense harm, and the major methods of minimizing
damage are prompt evacuation of the population, and
storm-proof buildings and shelters.

hybrid A type of plant or animal which has been cross-
bred from different varieties, usually to create a plant
which combines the characteristics of both parents. *High-
yielding varieties are hybrids.

hydraulic action The impact of moving water, which can
be a strong *erosive force. Hydraulic action is an important part of *marine and *river erosion, helping to create
*caves, *arches and *stacks, and cut away river *banks and
*plunge pools.

hydroelectric power Electricity generated by moving
water. The best locations for the generation of **hydroelectricity** are sites with rapidly moving rivers with a good,
year-round head of water, but hydroelectricity can also be
generated at the foot of *reservoirs or at *tidal *barrages.
Once the installation has been built, hydroelectric power-
stations have low running costs, and hydroelectricity is a
*renewable power source. There are, however, disadvan-
tages: reservoirs *silt up, populations have to be moved
from sites which are to be flooded, water-borne diseases
may increase, and there is some evidence that the construction of reservoirs increases the chance of earth movements. ▷ pumped storage scheme.

Hydrograph

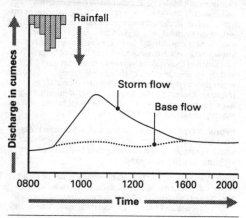

hydrograph A graph plotting the *discharge of a river over time. A hydrograph shows the time lag between the start of a rainstorm and the moment when the river begins to rise in response, and by studying hydrographs engineers can predict when flooding is likely to occur. The briefer the time lag and the taller the peak, the more likely a river is to flood. ▷ flood.

hydrological cycle The circling of water between the *atmosphere and the face of the earth. The major processes are *evaporation, the horizontal movement of *water vapour (*advection*), *condensation, *precipitation and *overland flow, and water can be stored in ice and snow, lakes and seas, and underground. The diagram

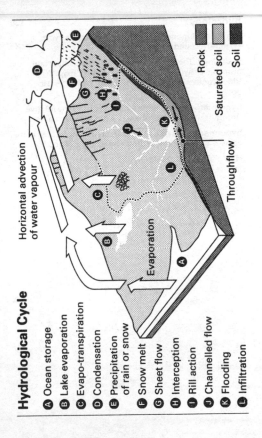

Hydrological Cycle

- A Ocean storage
- B Lake evaporation
- C Evapo-transpiration
- D Condensation
- E Precipitation of rain or snow
- F Snow melt
- G Sheet flow
- H Interception
- I Rill action
- J Channelled flow
- K Flooding
- L Infiltration

Horizontal advection of water vapour

Evaporation

Throughflow

above is a simplified model of a very complex cycle.
▷runoff, groundwater, infiltration. ✍

hydrology The study of the earth's water. Important branches of hydrology are *water supply, *irrigation, *flood control, and the generation of *hydroelectric power.

hygrometer An machine which measures the relative *humidity of the atmosphere. ▷whirling hygrometer.

hypermarket A large supermarket, usually located at the edge of a town or city, selling a huge range of goods.

HYV *high-yielding variety.

ice age A time in the history of the earth when *ice sheets were found in the mid-latitudes (the zones between 40˚ and 60˚ *latitude). The last time when ice sheets covered large parts of lowland Europe began 2 million years ago, and ended only 10 000 years before the present day. All of Britain north of a line from the Severn to the Thames *estuary was ice-covered during this period, which is known as the *Quaternary *glaciation. ▷ glacial erosion, glacial deposition, Little Ice Age.

ice-cap Essentially, an *ice sheet, but less than 50 000 km² in area. Examples are found in the Alps, or on islands, such as Iceland.

ice fall Part of a *glacier where the flow speeds up (perhaps as the *gradient gets steeper) and the ice is criss-crossed by *crevasses.

ice sheet A huge mass of ice, over 50 000 km² in area, and thicker in the middle than at the edges. (The Antarctic ice sheet is over 4 km thick at the centre.) Ice moves very slowly outwards, but with an unstoppable force.

igneous rock A rock formed from molten *magma, which has risen from deep within the earth's *crust and come near to the surface, forming an *intrusion. Because they do not reach the surface, igneous rocks cool slowly, so that crystals can separate out and become quite large. For this reason, igneous rocks are described as 'coarse-grained'. Granite is an igneous rock.

illiteracy Inability to read or write. Whereas *more developed countries have low **adult illiteracy rates**—the figure for the UK is under 1%—*less developed countries often have rates of 30% or more.

imbalance Inequality. In geography, the term is used to describe an unevenness in living standards and development across a country; this is often called a **regional imbalance**. Brazil is often quoted as an example of extreme regional imbalance. ▷ physical quality of life, Human Development Index.

IMF *International Monetary Fund.

immigration The permanent movement of people *into* a state; an **immigrant** is a person who moves into a country as a permanent resident. (Compare *emigration, *emigrant.) Most of the *more developed countries* have **immigration policies** by which they restrict the numbers of people coming in. Immigrants to Britain generally have to have family already living in the country, unless they are granted *political asylum. ▷ economic migrant, migration, plural society, pull factor, push factor.

imperialism The political control of one or a number of countries by a dominant state. ▷ colonialism, neo-colonialism, neo-imperialism.

impermeable Not allowing water to pass through. ▷ permeable. **Impermeable rocks** like *clay and *slate are watertight because they are not *porous.

impervious You may take this to mean *impermeable.

imports *Goods which are bought from a foreign country; these can be called **visible imports**. **Invisible imports** are services, like insurance, bought from outside a country. ▷ balance of payments.

import substitution Setting up *manufacturing industries within a *less developed country to avoid buying expensive foreign imports.

inaccessible Difficult to get to. Since transport costs are an important factor in many industries, inaccessible locations can be poor sites for development. ▷ peripheral, beta index.

incised meander A meander cut deep into a valley, with very steep banks; the incised meander at the foot of Durham Cathedral has *river cliffs over 20 m high. Incised meanders are cut when the river gains extra *erosive power, perhaps because it has been *rejuvenated. ▷ rejuvenation ▷▷ river erosion.

indigenous Belonging naturally to a region; for example, koala bears are indigenous to Australia. More recently, the term **indigenous people** has been used to describe the original inhabitants of an area, especially those peoples in possession before European *colonization. Europeans in the *New World and Australasia have treated indigenous peoples badly. Thousands were killed directly, or wiped out by European diseases like the common cold, or measles. Many now have high levels of alcoholism, and their ways of life are still under threat, notably in the development of Amazonia.

industrial Having to do with *industry. The **industrial revolution** is the period, in Britain from around 1780 to 1890, when many new inventions in *technology, most importantly the use of steam power, led to an enormous increase in *manufacturing. It was accompanied by rapid *urbanization, as thousands moved to new factories in towns and cities, and *coalfields became major growth areas.

industrial estate An area specially planned for industrial development, with plenty of space for building, and good transport links. Favourite locations are at the edge of *urban areas and near *motorways. ▷ science park.

industrial inertia The tendency of industries to remain in the same location even though the original reasons for their being there have gone. Pencils are still made in the Lake District although the industry no longer uses the graphite found there. Industrial inertia happens because the costs of relocating an industry can be too high.

industrialization The process of changing from a chiefly agricultural society, with small-scale, home-based *cottage industries to an industrial society, based on large-scale *manufacturing industry. As time passes there is usually a trend towards an increase in the importance of *service industry. Industrialization has often been seen as a solution to the problems of poverty in *less developed countries, perhaps because the richer states are all **industrialized countries**. However, industrialization can bring problems of *pollution, and, as in the case of Brazil, it often only benefits the rich. ▷ newly industrializing countries.

industrial location Industries are commonly established where transport costs—both of the *raw material to the factory and of the finished product to the *market—are as low as possible. In the past, in addition to closeness to raw materials and to markets, the major *factors influencing industrial location have been the cost of the site, government help (see *assisted area), a suitable labour force, port facilities, and good transport links. The latter are still very significant, but more recently, firms have been attracted by *greenfield sites, research facilities, high *amenity, and good facilities, like shops, housing, and schools, for the work-force. ▷ business park, footloose industry, psychic income, science park.

industry Nowadays, this term can be used to include any form of *economic activity, such as the 'football industry' or the 'pop music industry'. Economists and geographers tend to divide industry into four classes. **Primary industry** is the removal of *raw materials without processing them; examples include *mining, *forestry, and *fishing. **Secondary industry** is *manufacturing industry, and covers

all types of goods from food to electronics. The term
*heavy industry describes secondary industries producing
large, weighty goods, like railway lines. **Tertiary industry**
encompasses all the *service industries, including the
*warehousing, transporting and selling of goods, health,
education, and so on. **Quaternary industry** is a relatively
recent term, and describes the sale of advice and information; examples include teaching and investment consultancies.

infant mortality rate The number of deaths per thousand of children in their first year of life. Infant mortality
rates are a good indication of *living standards; rates for
*less developed countries are around 120 per thousand
while *more developed countries have rates close to 15 per
thousand. ▷ development indicators.

infiltration The movement of water into *soil or *porous
rocks. The **infiltration capacity** of a rock or soil, that is,
the rate at which infiltration happens, depends on how
dry it is, how porous it is, and how much water lies on top
of it.

informal employment An 'unofficial' job, where the
worker is not registered with the tax authorities and has
no sort of labour rights, or regular hours. In the **informal
economy**, which is also called the **informal sector**,
people make a living by shoe-shining, street hairdressing,
selling single cigarettes, or even queueing, or by illegal
activities like drug-dealing and prostitution. These types
of activity are very common in the cities of the *Third
World where up to 40% of jobs are in the informal sector.
Some people would like to see these workers brought into
the *formal sector, if only to make them pay income tax.

information technology The use of electronic equipment, such as computers and word-processors to store,
handle, and transmit information. ▷ post-industrial country.

infrastructure The pattern of communication and transport links, power supplies, administrative, health, education, and other services necessary for *economic development.

inner city The part of the city which is adjacent to the *central business district. Governments in many of the *more developed countries are now concerned with the problems of **inner city decline**, since these are often areas of old, run-down, and overcrowded housing, *derelict land, and failing industry. In some cases, the response to inner city problems has beeen *slum clearance and the building of tower blocks or the relocation of the inner city population at the edge of the city. Sometimes the inner city has been revitalized by unprompted *gentrification, and, increasingly, planners are establishing schemes for *urban renewal. ▷▷ urban morphology, ▷ twilight zone.

inorganic Describing any form of matter that has never lived and does not contain carbon.

input Anything that goes into an operation—money, materials, labour, and so on—and which is needed to bring about a desired *output. Inputs and outputs can be shown in the form of a flow diagram; here is one:

input	'plant'	output
climate soils fertilizer seed labour machinery	→ field →	crop

If the cost of the inputs is higher than the value of the output, the operation is uneconomic.

insecticide Any chemical used to kill insects. Insecticides are widely used in modern farming, but there is concern that they may kill harmless, or even useful insects, that they may get into the water supply and that these poisons may enter the *food chain and damage other organisms. The insecticide DDT eventually caused certain bird species to lay thin-shelled or infertile eggs with a catastrophic effect on bird populations. It is now officially banned, but is still used in some *Third World countries.

insolation The amount of *solar energy reaching the earth's surface. Insolation varies according to the season and to the latitude, because low-angled rays of the sun are less concentrated than high-angled rays.

Insolation

Two rays of the same size strike the Earth

integrated steelworks An industrial complex where every process needed to turn iron *ore into steel takes place on one site, thus saving transport costs.

intensive Describing a system where sizeable *inputs are used, usually to bring about large *outputs. From this stem terms like **labour intensive**—describing an activity which needs many workers; and **capital intensive**—

describing an activity which requires heavy *capital inputs. **Intensive farming** is characterized by heavy use of *fertilizers and pesticides and by high yields per hectare. **Intensively farmed** land in East Anglia can yield six times more grain per hectare than fields farmed *extensively.

interception The holding of raindrops by plants. When the plant can hold no more, the rain trickles down the plant stem. Interception lessens the impact of rain on the soil, thus helping to prevent soil erosion, and the fact that water is held by the plant lessens the risk of flooding.

interdependence The interlocking, or meshing, of the different parts of a system. For example, a *more developed country may depend on the *raw materials of a *less developed country just as much as the latter needs the *technology or *capital of the former.

interest The amount of extra money a borrower has to pay in return for being granted a loan. **Interest rates** are usually stated as percentages; an *annual interest rate of 5% means that the borrower has to pay $5 each year for every $100 borrowed. The rise in interest rates in the 1980s helped to bring about the *debt crisis.

interlocking spurs A series of ridges of land protruding alternately from either side of a valley, with the river winding between them. ▷▷ river features.

intermediate technology Although you may see this term used to mean *appropriate technology, this is not the exact meaning. Intermediate technology lies at a level somewhere between the very simple and the extremely complex, as in the table below:

Simple technology	Intermediate technology	High technology
Digging stick, or hoe	**Ox plough**	Tractor
Well	**Diesel pump**	Piped water
Watering-can	*trickle irrigation	Rotating sprayer

A tractor would be a piece of high technology appropriate to an advanced economy, and an ox plough a piece of intermediate technology appropriate to a *less developed country.

internal Inside; within. In *physical geography, an **internal process** is one which takes place within the earth; underneath the *crust. The term includes the processes connected with *folding, *faulting, *mountain building, *plate tectonics, and *vulcanicity. ▷magma.

international Concerning more than one, or many, or all, nations. **International trade** is the transference of goods between nations; this can be made more difficult if countries charge import taxes (*tariffs) or set *quotas. If the value of a state's *imports is more than that of its *exports, it will have a negative *balance of payments. ▷General Agreement on Tariffs and Trade.

international date line If it is noon at the Greenwich *meridian (0° longitude), it will be 12 midnight on the *same day* at 180° East, and 12 midnight on the *day before* at 180° West of Greenwich. However 180° West and 180° East are the same line of longitude. To adjust to this problem the line of longitude 180° has been established as the International Date Line, except where the meridian crosses land (see illustration). As travellers move from east to west across the Date Line, they lose a day—for example, if they cross on a Wednesday, they will have to go straight to Friday. As they move from west to east, they 'gain' a day—for example, if they cross on a Tuesday, the next day will also be Tuesday. Surprisingly enough, this works, and the dates never conflict, however much you cross the Date Line.

international division of labour See labour.

International Monetary Fund (IMF) An *international reserve of money held by the World Bank. Nations with cash to spare pay into the fund, and can decide how the money is to be used; the strength of their votes depends on the amount they pay in. The money is then loaned to countries in financial difficulties.

interrelated Jointly connected. Geographers are interested in many **interrelationships**, such as the links between *greenhouse gases and *industrialization or the *less developed and *more developed worlds. ▷interdependence.

intertropical convergence zone (ITCZ) A major *front occurring within the *tropics, where a dry *air mass meets a moist air mass. Rain forms at the front, and as the ITCZ moves with the seasons, the belt of rain also moves. The

Intertropical convergence zone (ITCZ)

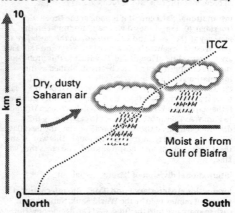

movements of the ITCZ are very unpredictable the further
it moves from the equator; in many years, regions which
depend on the convergence zone for rain receive none
because the zone has not moved far enough from the
equator.   ✍

intervening opportunities, theory of This 'law' of
*migration states that the numbers of people migrating to
a destination falls according to the number of 'opportunities', such as jobs which are found between their point of
origin and their destination. It is usually shown as: ✍

Intervening opportunities

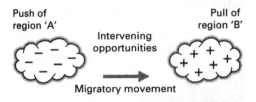

Push of   Pull of
region 'A'   region 'B'
                    Intervening
                    opportunities

                    Migratory movement

---

intrusion A mass of *magma which has risen from deep
below the earth's crust and 'squeezed' through cracks and
*faults in the rocks above. Intrusions produce many fea-
tures in the landscape, including *batholiths, *bosses,
*dykes, *tors, and *sills. Compare with *extrusion. An
intrusive rock is one which has made up an intrusion;
*granite is one.   ✍

invasion The movement of a new social group into an
area of a city. In the *inner cities, it has often been *immigrant groups, who are less worried by cramped conditions,

who have been the 'invaders', but *gentrification is also a form of invasion.

inverse distance, law of This 'law' of *migration states that the numbers of people migrating to a destination falls according to the increasing distance between their place of origin and their destination. It can be expressed as an equation:

$$n = \frac{1}{d}$$

where n = number of migrants
d = distance over which migration occurs.

Intrusion

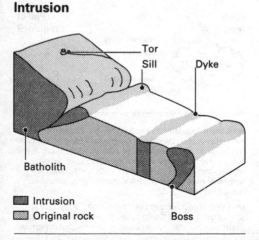

Inversion

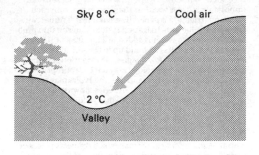

inversion of temperature A situation where air temperatures *rise* with height. (This is the reverse of the more common situation in which air cools with height.) Inversions occur when strong night-time radiation cools the earth's surface which then chills the air which is in contact with the ground, and when cold air flows into valley floors, pushing warmer air upwards. Inversions are very stable and damp or polluted air is often trapped below them. ✍

invisible exports *exports.

inward investment financial *investment in a *less developed country made by a *transnational corporation (multinational company), such as Nestlé or Ford. Transnational corporations are attracted to developing countries because of low labour costs or *free trade zones. Unfortunately, most of the profits from inward investment go to the transnational corporations.

irrigation The supply of water to the land by means such as channels, streams, lifting apparatus, hosepipes, and sprinklers. Without irrigation, *arable farming is usually impossible in areas with less than 250 mm of rain each year, and irrigation is generally advisable if *annual rainfall is under 500 mm. Irrigation systems can run into problems. If too much water is added in a hot area, or if the water is *saline, salts can build up in the soil and make crop-growing impossible. Large-scale irrigation schemes are expensive, the technology may not be *appropriate to *less developed countries, and the *reservoirs may trap useful *alluvium and *silt up. Fisheries *downstream may suffer, as the fish depend on the silt. In addition, if the scheme uses a river which crosses into another country, there may be arguments about who has the right to the water. ▷ tank irrigation, trickle irrigation.

isobar A line on a weather map which connects places of equal *atmospheric pressure. The pattern of the isobars can often reveal weather systems like *anticyclones and *depressions. The closer together the isobars, the stronger the winds will be. ▷▷ synoptic chart.

isochrone A line on a map which connects places of equal journey time from the same place of origin. Since *distance can also be measured in terms of travelling time, isochrones can indicate how 'far away' a place is.

isohyet A line on a map which connects places of equal rainfall within a given time span.

isoline A line on a map which connects places of equal value for some factor, such as *atmospheric pressure, *rainfall, journey time, or average *temperature. To construct an isoline:

(i) Plot the available data *in pencil* on a base map.
(ii) Decide on which value(s) you want for the line(s). If you are drawing more than one line, decide on the interval between lines.

Isochrone

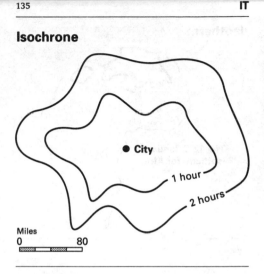

(iii) Use the values you have got to *extrapolate* the values you need.
(iv) Join the lines of equal value. ▷ contour, isobar, isochrone, isohyet, isotherm.

isotherm A line on a map which connects places of equal average temperature over a given period. ✍

isthmus A narrow strip of land, such as the isthmus of Panama, connecting two larger land areas.

IT *intermediate technology.

Isotherm

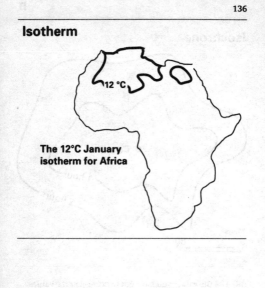

12 °C

The 12°C January
isotherm for Africa

J

joint A crack in a rock, but where there is no evidence of the rocks on either side having shifted along it (compare *fault). Some rocks, like *granite and *limestone are very strongly **jointed**, and their joints are lines of weakness which are more easily *eroded than the rest of the rock. ▷ cave, karst, tor.

jungle In geography, this is a precise term, referring to the vegetation which develops after an area of untouched *tropical rain forest has been cleared.

K

kame An isolated hill or mound of sands and gravels which have been deposited by glacial *meltwater. Many seem to be the old *deltas of *sub-glacial streams. ▷▷ fluvio-glacial.

karst An area of *limestone which is dominated by underground streams, hollows, and pits. Some *limestones are *porous, all are *permeable, and all are easily attacked by rainwater, which is *acid, because of the *atmospheric *carbon dioxide which is naturally dissolved in it. Typical features of **karst scenery** include *caves, *gorges, and *swallow holes. The classic area of karst is in the former Yugoslavia, from where it gets its name, but small-scale karst can be seen in the UK in places like Malham Tarn, Yorkshire, or Cheddar, Somerset. 🖉

Karst

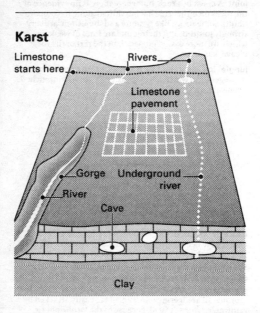

Limestone starts here

Rivers

Limestone pavement

Gorge

Underground river

River

Cave

Clay

kettle hole A small hollow on the surface of a *moraine or *outwash plain, often filled with water. It formed when a large block of *glacier ice, which was originally embedded in the *drift, melted (but any water in the kettle hole is not from the original ice block!).

kilo- Prefix representing 1000, hence **kilogram**, a weight of 1000 grams (approximately equivalent to 2.2 lb), and **kilometre**, a distance of 1000 metres (approximately equivalent to 0.62 mile).

knick point, nick point A point at which there is a sudden *break of slope in the long profile of a river. ▷▷ river features.

L

labour In geography and economics, this term refers to the work-force. Labour is important in most industries; some, such as electronics, require **skilled labour**, others, like road-sweeping, use **unskilled labour**. Classifications of employment distinguish between **manual labour**, where the work is very physical, and **non-manual labour**. Many industries are attracted by **cheap labour**, and this is a reason for many *transnational corporations to *locate in *less developed countries. Often, TNCs operate an *international division of labour; research and development is carried out in the *more developed countries, and unskilled operations in the *LDCs. Those industries which rely on workers rather than machinery are said to be

labour intensive. Labour-intensive industries can suit less developed countries very well, since unemployment in such countries is often high, and more jobs are created in labour-intensive enterprises than in highly mechanized industries.

lacustrine To do with *lakes.

lagged flow The increased flow of a river once it has begun to respond to a fall of rain. ▷hydrograph.

lagoon A *bay which is totally or partially enclosed by a *spit.

lake A sheet of water, found inland. Natural lakes occur in hollows on the earth's surface, and most will eventually disappear as they become filled with alluvium dropped by rivers flowing into the lake.

land breeze A wind blowing *from* the land *to* the sea. Although the land is warmer than the sea during the day,

Land breeze: evening

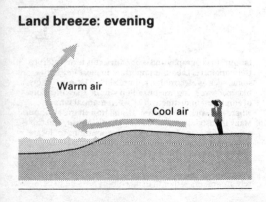

Warm air

Cool air

by evening the sea is warmer than the land (the sea heats and cools much more slowly than the land). This means that the air above the sea is warmer than the air above the land. The warm sea air rises, and air above the land flows seawards to take its place. ▷ sea breeze.   ✍

land consolidation A change in the ownership of *fragmented land. A *fragmented farm is inefficient to run, and many governments have tried to solve this problem by *land reform.

landfill site A large hollow in the ground, often an old quarry, into which rubbish is tipped.

landform A *physical feature of the earth's crust, such as a *valley, a *spur, or a *mountain. The study of landforms is *geomorphology.

land invasion The occupation of land, often by force, and generally illegally, although the new 'owners' are often left in peace. Land invasions have been common in Latin America, where the systems of *land tenure are very unfair to the poor, especially the *indigenous people (compare *invasion).

land reform A change in the ownership of land (*land tenure). In many countries, a few, powerful landowners held large estates while their workers had little or no land of their own. Some of the governments of these countries have tried to redistribute the land by buying the estates and selling sections of them to the *peasants. Land reforms have operated, for example, in Peru and the *Mezzogiorno* of southern Italy, but in both cases they have not been as helpful as expected to the peasants; because other factors have worked against the new owners, because the new parcels of land were not big enough, or because the schemes were badly planned. A different type of land reform takes place in *land consolidation.

landscape The face of the earth. The **physical landscape** is the landscape unaltered by man—although it is increasingly rare to find unaltered landscapes—and the **human landscape** is the landscape as influenced by human activity.

landscape evaluation An attempt to assess the landscape in objective terms. Sometimes many opinions are sounded out so that outstandingly beautiful landscapes can be identified. (See *Area of Outstanding Natural Beauty.) Attempts have even been made to put a cash value on a landscape, but, of course, people's preferences vary. ▷ cost–benefit analysis, environmental impact assessment.

land set aside *set aside.

landslide A rapid downslope movement of a volume of soil and/or rock. Landslides occur when the material on a slope becomes unstable—perhaps because the soil or rock has become saturated, or because it has been undercut at the base of the slope. ▷▷ mass movement.

land tenure The way in which land is held. The most common systems are *owner-occupancy, where the landowner lives on his land, tenancies, where the tenant pays rent in cash for the land, and *sharecropping, where the tenant pays a proportion of his crop as rent to the landlord. Other systems include collective farms, *plantations, and *common land. ▷ housing tenure.

land use Any use made by man of a section of land. **Land use maps** in the UK show 256 categories, but the basic ones are *agricultural, *industrial, *recreational, *residential, transport, and *woodland. **Land use conflicts** are common—the UK Department of Transport often faces opposition when it wants to build a motorway over a beauty spot or *Site of Special Scientific Interest, but there have been many cases where developers have been allowed to build in the *green belt.

Land value gradient

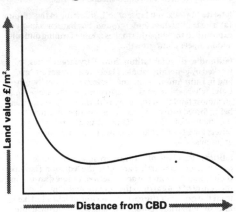

land value gradient The change in the value of land across a *central place , whether expressed in cost or rental value per square metre or per hectare. In a typical city in the *developed world, land values are high at the centre (the *CBD), falling with movement outwards, but rising in the *suburbs, where amenity value is higher. ▷bid rent, competition.

lapse rate Generally speaking, the air becomes cooler as you climb upwards (but see inversion). The speed with which the temperature falls is the lapse rate. Lapse rates vary according to the amount of water vapour in the air.

lateral At the side. **Lateral erosion** occurs at the banks on each side of a river (vertical erosion), and **lateral**

*moraines are found along the sides of a valley. ▷▷ river erosion, glacial deposition. ▷ medial moraine.

laterite A thick, red layer of soil, occurring in the *tropics. Laterite is soft when underground, but hardens rapidly on exposure to the soil—this makes *arable farming difficult, and hampers plant growth.

latifundia, singular **latifundium** Very large estates, worked by generally landless labourers. Wages are low, and in Latin America and the *Mezzogiorno* region (southern Italy), where these estates were common, the workers had an almost feudal relationship with the landowner, often being forced into compulsory labour, or being fined for the smallest of offences. Many latifundia still exist, but others have been broken up under *land reform programmes.

latitude Parallels of latitude are imaginary circles drawn across the earth, parallel to the *equator. They take their numbers from the angle between a line drawn from the centre of the earth to the equator and a line drawn from the centre of the earth to the line of latitude. Like lines of *longitude, parallels of latitude are divided into minutes (shown thus ′ in atlases) and seconds (shown thus ″), with 60 minutes to a degree and 60 seconds to a minute. Using these two lines as *coordinates, it is possible to locate any position on earth.   ✍

Laurasia A 'supercontinent', formed when *Pangaea split, and composed of what are now North America, Greenland, Europe, and northern Asia. ▷▷ continental drift, plate tectonics. Laurasia broke up around 100 million years ago, when North America was detached from Europe.

lava *Magma which has escaped from beneath the earth's crust and has flowed on to the surface. Many magma flows contain water; if the water vaporizes it will explode, causing particularly violent *volcanic *eruptions. **Acid lava,**

Latitude

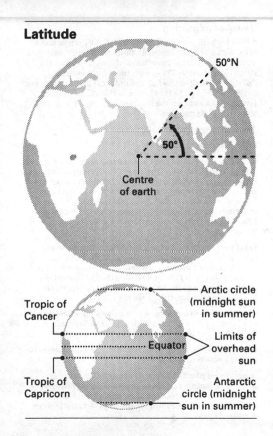

with a high silica content, is *viscous* ('sticky'), while **basic lava**, with a low silica content, flows more freely, and thus makes up most of the **lava flows** which spread over the surface of the earth. These sometimes form **lava *plateaus**; more or less flat, upland areas of solidified lava (an example is the Snake Plateau in the USA); but most lava flows spread over the sea floor, welling up from constructive *plate margins.

'laws' of migration See migration.

LDC *less developed country.

leaching The washing out of soil minerals as water moves down through the soil. This lessens the fertility of the soil, especially in *tropical areas, where chemical reactions are much stronger. In the *developed world, fertilizers are leached from the soil, and drain into the rivers, often entering the water supply , or causing *eutrophication. Leaching is an important process in the formation of *soil horizons.

least cost location Costs—including transport, labour, site, and so on—are an important factor in *industrial location. A least cost location is where total costs are at a minimum. In theory, it is possible to determine the least cost location for transport costs alone by using a triangle of location; in practice, things are not so simple.

least developed country A particularly poor *less developed country. Examples include Chad and Bangladesh. ▷development indicators, data file, Third World.

lee The side (**lee side**), sheltered from the wind. **Leeward** means towards the lee side.

leguminous plant Any plant which can 'fix' nitrogen from the atmosphere, that is, that can extract nitrogen from the air, turn it into nitrates (which are important fertilizers) and therefore improve the soil's fertility. ▷green manure, organic.

less developed country (LDC) Any country with a low
*per capita *GNP, a poor industrial base, high employment
in agriculture, and heavily dependent on the export of
unprocessed goods. Less developed countries are also
dependent on some form of *aid, or outside finance.
▷IMF. Examples include Jamaica and Ghana. ▷develop-
ment indicators, data file, more developed country, newly
industrializing country.

levée A raised bank of *alluvium at the side of a river.
Levées form naturally, when a river overflows its banks,
because the rate of flow decreases, so that silt is deposited.
In time, the river may be higher than the surrounding
countryside. Levées may also be constructed artificially to
cut down the risk of *flooding. ▷▷ river features.

leverage Using public (tax-payers') money to invest in an
area, like London's Docklands or the Cardiff Bay Area, to
attract private investment (developers) into the area.

ley Grassland deliberately planted by a farmer. Ley grass
can be used to make *silage, and is often an important part
of a *rotation.

life expectancy The average number of years a person
can expect to live. Figures for life expectancy can be given
for regions, or for whole countries. In the UK, life expectancy decreases with employment status; partly because
manual jobs are more dangerous than non-manual, partly
because of differences in life-style—particularly in eating
habits. World-wide life expectancy is linked with *development; average life expectancy for a *less developed country is around 50 years, while for a *more developed
country it is around 75 years. Among other things, this
reflects the high *infant mortality rates in *LDCs. Life
expectancy is a particularly good *development indicator
because it reflects many of the factors which make up the
*physical quality of life—housing, health, education, sani-

tation, nutrition, and so on. In the *demographic transition model, life expectancy rises as the *death rate falls.

light industry Any industry producing goods that are light in weight and relatively high in value; electrical goods are good examples. Light industries are often to be found on *industrial estates.

lignite A soft, brown form of coal, which does not burn with as much heat as the more usual, black, form because it contains less carbon.

limb The section of a *fold on either side of the central axis.

limestone Any rock made of calcium carbonate, including *chalk. Many are formed from the fossils of minute *marine organisms. A **limestone pavement** is a more or less horizontal, bare limestone surface, cut into by *grykes (*clint). Limestones are *permeable, and thus rivers do not flow over them (but see *dry valley). This means that even soft limestones, like chalk, form uplands because there is little erosion from *overland flow or *river erosion. However, they are easily attacked along their *joints by rainwater, which is *acid, because of the *atmospheric *carbon dioxide which is naturally dissolved in it, so that they often show the features of *karst scenery.

linear Of, or along, a line. **Linear settlement** is a long, narrow line of buildings, often along a road (*ribbon development *settlement pattern). A **linear scale** is the diagram

---

Linear scale

Kilometres

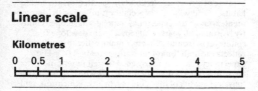

Linear patterns in the Cascade Mts

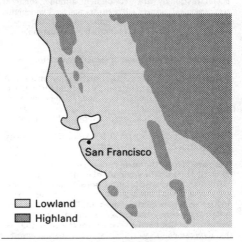

○ Lowland
■ Highland

on a map which indicates the length on the ground of any distance shown on the map. Many *mountain ranges show a distinct **linear pattern**.

link The *route joining two *nodes, or places. ▷ accessibility.

listed building A building thought to be so architecturally outstanding that it cannot be altered or demolished without express permission. Even changing the front door can lead to a fine, and an order to change it back. ▷ conservation area.

literacy The ability to read and write. **Literacy rates** record the percentage of adults who are **literate**; and these *correlate strongly with *development, although some *less developed countries, like Nicaragua, have very high rates. Increasing literacy is the aim of many *LDCs, because a literate work-force is much more adaptable. ▷development indicators.

lithosphere The outermost layer of the earth; the *crust.

Little Ice Age The time period, roughly between AD 1550 and 1850, when temperatures in Europe and North America were lower than they are now, and *glaciers advanced. In Britain, it was not unusual for the Thames to freeze over; 'ice fairs' were held, with oxen roasted on the ice.

livestock Animals, such as cattle, oxen, sheep, and goats, kept by farmers. ▷ pastoral farming.

living standards The quality of a person's life is very much tied up with the **standard of living** enjoyed. The most basic factors are education, housing, health, income, employment, and sanitation but *amenity and *environmental *pollution are also important. The UN *Human Development Report* lists dozens of factors, and, using a sophisticated statistical procedure, concluded, in 1991, that living standards were highest in Canada and lowest in Guinea. ▷ Human Development Index, physical quality of life.

load The material carried by any agent of *erosion (water, ice, or wind), although the term is mostly used in connection with rivers. The ability of a river to carry its load depends on the volume and speed of flow (*discharge). If either decreases, the river will drop some of its load, starting with the heaviest material first (*deposition). A river's load is carried in *solution* (dissolved material), in *suspension* (material 'hanging' in the water), or as *bed load* (material rolled along the bed).

local climate The weather conditions in a small area. Sometimes the weather can vary more between the city and the countryside than it does nationally. This is because the city can be seen as a *heat island, where temperatures are higher through man's activities; cars, trains, factories, houses, and offices all give out heat, so that the *CBD can be degrees warmer than a nearby *rural area. High buildings can create a wind-tunnel effect. The weather in forested areas also differs from that of the open country, and clearing a forest can change the local climate.

locality Place.

location The place where a feature is found. Geographers are interested in **locational analysis**, which takes two forms: explaining why something—a town, a suburb, or a woodland, for example—is found where it is; or working out where best to locate a new development, such as a shopping centre, hospital, or factory. ▷ industrial location.

location quotient A statistic calculated to show the relative importance of an activity, such as car manufacturing or university lecturing, in a particular place. It can be worked out using the following formula:

$$\frac{\text{\% employed in activity within a region}}{\text{\% employed nationally in the same activity}}$$

A location quotient of 3 for lecturers in Oxford, for example, shows that Oxford has three times the national average of university teachers.

loess A fine, yellow, wind-blown, fertile soil.

longitude Lines of longitude, also known as 'meridians', are imaginary circles drawn around the earth in a north–south direction. A meridian takes its number from the horizontal angle between a line drawn from the centre

Longitude

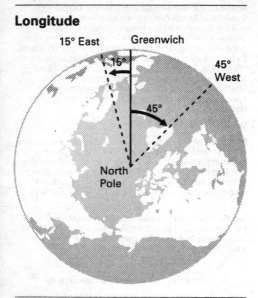

of the earth to the longitude 0˚ (the Greenwich meridian) and a line drawn from the centre of the earth to the meridian itself. Like lines of *latitude, meridians of longitude are divided into minutes (shown thus ' in atlases) and seconds (shown thus "), with 60 minutes to a degree and 60 seconds to a minute. Using these two lines as *coordinates, it is possible to locate any position on earth. Lines of longitude are examples of *great circles. ▷coordinates.

longshore drift The movement of *sand and shingle along a coast. Waves usually surge up a beach at an oblique angle, but drain back seawards at a right angle. The sediment carried by the waves also takes this zig-zag course, and the net result is a movement of the sediment along the beach. **Longshore drift features** include *spits, *bars and *tombolos. ▷▷ marine deposition.

low A shorter term for an area of low *atmospheric pressure (anything below about 996 *mb); in other words, for a *depression.

low order Describing a *good or *service which is provided even where the potential market (*threshold population) is quite small. Low-order goods and services tend to be items which people buy frequently, like newspapers or haircuts and they are thus found very frequently, even in quite small settlements. ▷ range of a good, threshold.

lumbering The felling of trees.

M

magma The molten rock found below the earth's *crust. It can pierce into the crust to form *intrusions of *igneous rock, but if it escapes on to the surface it is called lava. ▷batholith, dyke, sill, volcano. ▷▷igneous.

malnutrition A disorder suffered by someone whose diet does not contain all the foods necessary for good health. ▷deficiency disease, undernourishment.

Malthus Thomas Malthus was an English clergyman, very interested in population growth. In 1783, he published his theory, also known as **malthusianism**, which stated that whereas food supply grew *arithmetically, population increased geometrically. He predicted that population would soon naturally outstrip food supply with a number of consequences, which are known as **malthusian checks**: *misery*, which included famine, disease, and war; *vice*, which included the killing of babies; and *moral restraint*, which included celibacy and late marriage. Malthus's predictions did not come true because agricultural productivity improved and new lands were found to colonize. Food supplies seemed to be adequate. Furthermore, *birth rates fell in the *more developed countries. However, many today believe in **neo-malthusianism**—the conviction that Malthus is finally being proved right—because of the dramatic population increases of the last 50 years. ▷ birth rate.   ✍

mantle The middle layer of the earth, lying between the *crust and the *core. It is around 2800 km thick, and consists of *magma. ▷▷crust.

Malthus

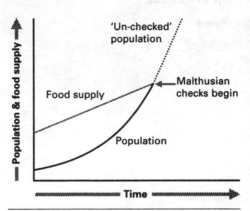

manual Done by hand, rather than entirely by machine. This would make using a pneumatic drill **manual labour**, even though a piece of machinery is used.

manufacturing The making of goods. In geography, the term **manufacturing industry** refers to factory goods rather than to handicrafts. An alternative term for manufacturing industry is *secondary industry.

map A representation on a flat surface of all, or part of the earth. No map shows every feature, and specialized maps, such as *land use maps or *density shading maps are widely available. When maps of a small area are made, the problem of putting a curved area on to a flat sheet does not really arise, but when maps of large areas of the earth

Map projection

Peters

Mercator

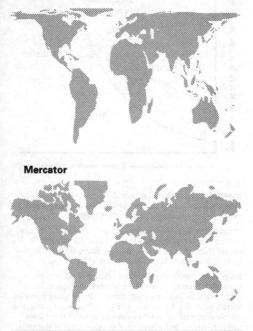

are made the problem becomes acute. (Try peeling an orange without breaking up the peel, and squashing the whole peel flat without doubling it up, and you will see the problem.) Essentially, map-makers (cartographers) have a choice: either the area of a country shown on a map will be correct, or the shape will be right, but they cannot have both. Different **map projections** are used, and this explains why some maps of the earth look very different from others. The **Mercator projection** shows the land masses in their correct shape, but wrong area; the **Peters projection** shows them with their correct area, but wrong shape. See also topological map.   ✍

maquis A shrubby, evergreen type of vegetation found in southern France.

marble A hard, crystalline rock, shot through with veins of different coloured minerals. It is a valuable building stone, and is a *metamorphic rock which originally formed as *limestone.

marginal Barely adequate or provided for; the term **marginalized** describes people who are not provided for, or not considered to be important. **Marginal land** is land which, in economic terms, is not worth farming. Most hill farms in the EC are marginal. Some governments subsidize the farming of marginal land in order to keep farmers' livelihoods secure.

marine Connected with the sea (but see also maritime). **Marine erosion** is erosion by the sea, and the main processes involved are *abrasion, *hydraulic action, and *solution. Important features of marine erosion include *bays, *caves, *cliffs, *headlands, *arches, *stacks, and *wave-cut (abrasion) platforms.   ✍
   Marine deposition occurs when material transported by *longshore drift, such as *sand and shingle, is dropped, often in a more sheltered area. Important features of marine deposition include *beaches, *spits, *bars, and

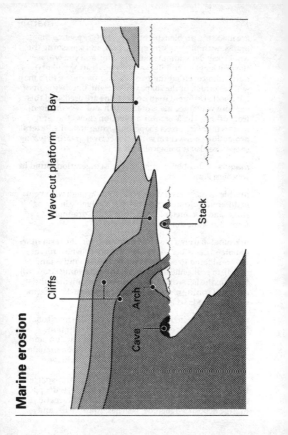

Marine erosion

Bay

Wave-cut platform

Stack

Cliffs

Arch

Cave

Marine deposit

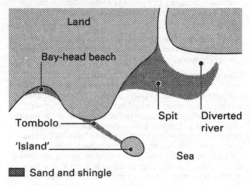

Land

Bay-head beach

Tombolo

'Island'

Spit

Diverted river

Sea

▨ Sand and shingle

marine deposition include *beaches, *spits, *bars, and *tombolos.

maritime Connected with the sea. *Marine has the same meaning, but, in geography, maritime is used to describe *climates and marine is used to describe *landforms and *landscape processes. A **maritime climate** is one strongly influenced by the sea, which moderates temperature changes and keeps air humid. (▷ humidity). Maritime climates are to be found in most regions within about 50 miles (80 km) of the sea. Temperatures are moderate, the *annual temperature range is small, and annual rainfall is generally above 600 mm.

market In geography and economics, the demand for a good and/or service. It is not enough to have people who require a good; to make up a market, they also have to be able to pay for the good. The **market area** is the area from which consumers will travel to buy a *good or *service. Generally speaking, the larger the *central place, the larger the market area. ▷ central place theory, location theory.

market forces The forces of supply and demand. The **market economies** of the world are the capitalist countries of the world.

market garden An area of land given over to the commercial production of fruit, flowers, and vegetables. **Market gardening** traditionally took place where demand was high—for example near large towns and cities—or where the climate was especially favourable, as in the Vale of Evesham, or the South-West peninsula. With improvements in transport, and with the introduction of frozen foods, more distant areas have been able to move to market gardening. East Anglia, for example, now specializes in frozen peas, and strawberries flown in from Kenya are quite common in British supermarkets. Most market gardening is both *capital intensive and *labour-intensive.

market town In Britain, in historical times, towns had to be granted the right to hold a market by the crown. Those towns with a charter to hold a market once a week, or more often, were market towns, and became more important *central places than those without a charter.

marl A mixture of clay and lime (calcium carbonate). **Marling** is the addition of lime to heavy clay land to make it lighter for arable farming.

mass movement The movement of rock fragments and soil down a slope, under the influence of gravity. At one extreme, there are *landslides which are very rapid; at the other, there is *soil creep, which is almost imperceptible, and there are many types of movement between these two. Mass movement occurs when the material on a slope becomes unstable—perhaps because the soil or rock has

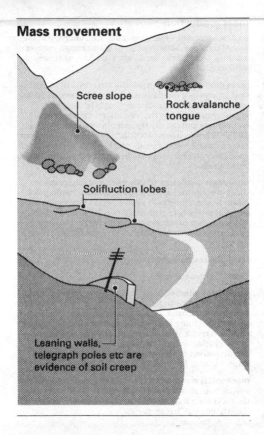

Mass movement

Scree slope

Rock avalanche tongue

Solifluction lobes

Leaning walls, telegraph poles etc are evidence of soil creep

become saturated, or because it has been undercut at the base of the slope. Mass movement is also known as **mass wasting**. ▷ avalanche, landslide, mud flow, soil creep, solifluction. ✍

mass production The making of large quantities of identical articles by a standardized mechanical process. **Mass-produced** items are produced cheaply because the manufacturer can buy the *raw materials in bulk at a cheaper rate and can use the machinery to a maximum. All the different stages of production can be broken down into an assembly-line system, and the high *capital cost of machinery and buildings can be spread over a large number of goods.

maximum–minimum thermometer A thermometer which records the highest (**maximum**) and lowest (**minimum**) temperatures over a given period. One version uses a tube of mercury to push small needles along a column. When the mercury moves away, the needles remain at the furthest position it has reached. Magnets are used to reset the needles.

MDC *more developed country.

mean *arithmetic mean.

meander A winding curve in the course of a river. The outer bank of a meander generally slopes more steeply than the inside bank. This is because the water flow on the outer edge is more rapid than the water flow on the inner edge. As a result, we characteristically find erosion and *undercutting on the outer edge, forming a *river cliff, and deposition on the inner edge, forming a *slip-off slope. ▷▷ river features. ✍

mechanical weathering The breaking down of rocks *in situ* (without moving them) by purely physical processes—the rocks are not chemically altered. Processes include *exfoliation and *freeze–thaw.

Meander

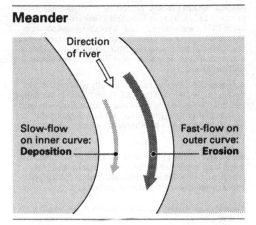

medial In the middle; a **medial moraine** is a *moraine found in the middle of a valley (compare *lateral moraine) A medial moraine was often formed when two *lateral moraines from two different valleys merged as the valleys met. ▷▷moraine.

median A number representing the central value of any set of figures. To find the median in a data set:

(i) Write out all the numbers in order of size.

(ii) If there is an odd number of figures, the figure at the centre of this list is the median. Thus, for the numbers 1, 3, 8, 10, and 11, the median is 8.

(iii) If there is an even number of figures, a number halfway between the two central figures is the median. Thus, for the numbers 2, 4, 5, 6, 8, and 9, the median is 5.5. See also arithmetic mean and mode.

Mediterranean climate A *climate of hot (average temperature 22 ˚C), dry summers, and warm (average temperature 12 ˚C), wet winters; rainfall totals around 650 mm. This climate is not only characteristic of countries bordering on the Mediterranean Sea, but is also found in California, central Chile, southern Australia, and the extreme south of Africa.

megalopolis This word was originally used to describe the eastern seaboard of the USA, from Boston to Washington, but is now used for any more or less continuous built-up area of over 10 million inhabitants. A megalopolis usually forms when a number of *conurbations merge together.

meltwater Water given out when snow or ice melts. Meltwater is an important element in the rise in river *discharge in spring. **Glacial meltwater** comes from glaciers and is responsible for *fluvio-glacial features.

mental map A map within someone's mind, which may be very different from a real map. For example, when British people attempt to draw a map of the world, they may very well miss out many countries, like Latvia, for example, because they don't know where they are, or have never heard of them. In the same way, most English people, when drawing a map of Britain, make Scotland far too small, and many Londoners' mental maps of Britain have northern England full of coal-mines and terraced houses. It is important to understand how people see the world, because they are more strongly influenced by how they see the world than by how the world really *is*. ▷behavioural geography, perception.

mesa A steep-sided, upland *plateau, made of horizontal layers of rock, topped by a more resistant rock layer. Mesas are common in the deserts of the USA and Mexico, and are larger versions of *buttes. ▷▷ desert features.

metamorphism In geology, the change in the nature of a rock caused by intense heat and/or pressure:

Original rock	Metamorphic form
Limestone	Marble
Sandstone	Quartzite
Shale	Slate

Metamorphic rocks are hard, and resistant to erosion.

meteorology The study of the *atmosphere, especially of the *weather. **Meteorologists** study weather-forming processes and attempt to use their knowledge to forecast future weather.

microclimate The climate found in a very small area, such as one side of a building—which may be shadier or more sheltered than another—or within a forest.

mid-oceanic ridge An underwater section of the earth's *crust where *magma rises up through a cracking and widening ridge, creating new crust which is then pushed away from the ridge. These ridges are *constructive margins. ▷ plate tectonics.

migrant A person who moves, whether permanently, seasonally, or temporarily.

migration The permanent, seasonal or temporary movement of people.

A classification of migration, with examples:

International	{	Permanent: *Russians to the USA*
		Seasonal: *American farmworkers to Canada*
		Temporary: *holidaymakers*

Internal	{	Permanent: *workers moving to jobs in new places*
		Seasonal: *transhumance
		Temporary: *students*
		Daily: *commuters*

Many **laws of migration** have been put forward including the theory that migration is inversely proportion to distance:

$$m \propto \frac{1}{d} \text{ (see distance decay)}$$

and that migration between two settlements varies with the size of the two settlements and the distance between them—the *gravity model. A further 'law' concerns *intervening opportunities. The reasons for migration are *pushes—negative factors, like lack of land, which 'push' people from their homes; and *pulls—positive factors like better paid jobs, which attract people to new locations. ▷economic migrant, emigration, immigration, step migration, rural depopulation, urbanization.

mine An underground passage, dug in order to extract *minerals (but see also *opencast mining), from which we derive the word **mining**.

mineral Strictly speaking, any naturally occurring *inorganic material, although crude oil and coal are described as minerals. **Mineral ores**, like iron ore, are deposits within rocks which contain enough useful mineral content to be worth extracting.

mist A thin *fog, enabling you to see between 1 and 2 km.

mixed farm, mixed farming A type of agriculture where both *arable and *pastoral farming take place. The manure from the animals is used to improve the fertility of the soil and so increase crop yields (compare with *monoculture).

MNC multinational corporation. See transnational corporation.

mode The statistic which occurs most often in a data set. It is quoted to give some kind of average, representative value. To find the mode:

(i) Write out all the numbers in order of size.

(ii) Count how many times each number occurs.

(iii) The number occurring most often is the mode.

model A simplified image of some aspect of the real world, usually developed to aid our understanding. Models described in this dictionary include: Burgess model (concentric model), demographic transition model, gravity model, Hoyt model (sector model), multiple nuclei model, Myrdal model.

monoculture A farming system given over entirely, or almost entirely, to one product, for example, lavender growing in the south of France. Monoculture has the advantage of increasing efficiency, but leaves the farmer very vulnerable to price falls, *climatic hazards, and crop diseases, and monoculture without *rotation can bring about a loss in soil fertility, or even *soil erosion.

monsoon In the original Arabic, the word means 'seasonal wind'. More generally, it is used to describe the winds which, coming in from the sea, bring sudden, very heavy rain to South-East Asia in summer, and then switch direction, blowing outward from the land.

moor An area of open, unfarmed upland. Many moorlands, like Dartmoor and the Yorkshire Moors have *acid soils and *peat bogs are common.

moraine The stony landform (*till) left behind when a *glacier has melted and dropped its *load. Moraines are classified by their location. **Lateral moraines** are found at the sides of a valley, **medial moraines** run down the centre of a valley, and **terminal moraines** mark the end of the glacier. ▷▷ glacial deposition.

more developed country (MDC) A term used to describe a country where *living standards are high. The more developed countries are found in Europe and North America, but Japan, Australia, and New Zealand also fall into this category. *Development indicators are used to distinguish the more developed countries; typical 'scores' would be:

*Infant mortality rate	10/1000 or less
Daily *calorie intake	over 2200
*Literacy rate	c.99%
Percentage having secondary schooling	over 90%
Percentage of workers in agriculture	c.3%
Per capita electricity consumption/year	c.5000 kg coal equivalent
*Per capita *GNP	over $9000
*Birth rate	c.12/1000
*Death rate	c.12/1000
(1992 statistics)	

Alternative terms for more developed country are economically advanced country and economically developed country. When taken as a group, MDCs are referred to as 'the developed world' or *the North. ▷ less developed country, the South.

morphology Shape and structure, as in *urban morphology.

motorway A type of major road restricted to certain vehicles. Motorways are designed with no roundabouts or traffic lights, in order to speed-up road traffic. Since rapid transport is important to many companies, closeness to a motorway has become an important locational factor. This is particularly well illustrated by the British M4, which has become such a 'magnet' for offices and industry that it is known as the 'M4 corridor'.

mountain A naturally occurring, steep upland. There is no hard and fast opinion on the height at which a hill becomes a mountain; in Britain it might be about 300 m, but this would seem small in other countries. A **mountain**

range is an extensive stretch of mountains, often with the mountains arranged in a distinct *linear pattern. The process of mountain building is known as an *orogeny.

mouth The point at which a river meets the sea. ▷estuary.

mud flow A *mass movement downslope of liquefied clay. Mud flows are very fast-moving. They are triggered off by heavy rain; in 1966 a mud flow from a *spoil heap at Aberfan, South Wales, washed over a school, killing 116

Multiple nuclei

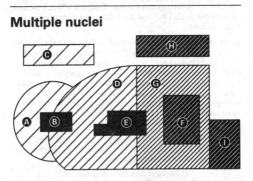

Ⓐ High-class housing   Ⓕ Light industry

Ⓑ Shopping-centre   Ⓖ Low-class housing

Ⓒ Residential suburb   Ⓗ Heavy industry

Ⓓ Middle-class housing   Ⓘ Industrial suburb

Ⓔ CBD

children, and in Japan in 1919 heavy rain caused *volcanic ash to turn into a mud flow, killing 5500 people.

multinational Occurring in more than one state, as in **multinational corporation (MNC)**, another term for *transnational corporation (but see multinational state).

multinational state A *state made up of more than one *nation.

multiple nuclei model A *model of *urban land use, showing that a city may grow from a number of separate centres, or nuclei. Growth occurs from each *nucleus, and in time the nuclei expand until they form a continuous built-up area. ✍

multiple use Many uses. In **multiple resource management**, this is the shared use of some asset by several different enterprises or activities, together with the aim of minimizing damage to that asset. For example, a *reservoir may be created to supply water to a city, but may also be used for fishing and water sports. The most common example of multiple resource management is **multiple land use**—the reservoir is a good example—but *capital may also be put to multiple uses.

multiplier effect A series of events, each one caused by the one before, and often working in a circle. The flow diagram below illustrates one example:

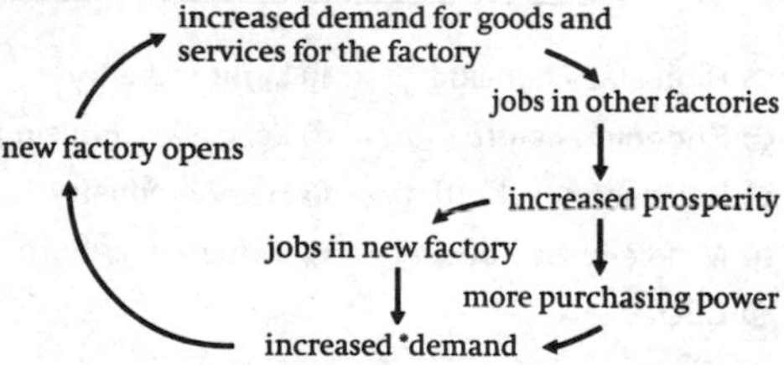

This is a *positive* example of the multiplier effect, but there are also *negative* examples:

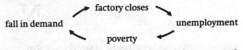

factory closes

fall in demand   unemployment

poverty

The idea of the multiplier effect lies behind the concept of *cumulative causation.

multi-purpose river project A scheme to dam a river in order to use the water in more than one way. Common purposes are to control flooding, produce *hydroelectric power, provide irrigation or supply water to a large urban area. The first major multi-purpose river project was set up by the Tennessee Valley Authority in the USA, where it revitalized an area of great poverty.

Myrdal model The *core–periphery model.

N

nation A large number of people of mainly common descent, language, and history. Although the words are used interchangeably, a nation need not be a *state, as there can be *multinational states. Yugoslavia was one.

National Grid The series of reference lines (or *coordinates) used on British *Ordnance Survey maps, and shown on the back of the 1 : 50 000 sheets.

National Park An area of such outstanding scenery that the government has put in place very strict checks on new development. In England and Wales, this protection is limited by the need for farmland, forestry, and other commercial uses, but there are fairly strict controls on new construction. New roads can be hidden under cut-and-cover tunnels or within cuttings, camping and caravan sites can be hidden behind trees, and new buildings have to be made of the same stone and to the same design as the older buildings. Some problems have surfaced since National Parks have been set up. The Parks are generally sited in areas with little industry. Since it is difficult to get permission to locate new industries in National Parks, local people may find it hard to find jobs. Furthermore, if the Park becomes overcrowded, as often happens, it may become less attractive to some visitors. One solution to this problem is to concentrate visitors in a few points served by car parks, gift shops, and information centres. These points are known as *honeypot sites. In this way, the rest of the park becomes less crowded. British National Parks were first planned in 1949, and now National Parks make up about 20% of the area of Britain. ▷▷ Area of Outstanding Natural Beauty.

National Rivers Authority (NRA) The organization which oversees the use, and the environmental health, of British rivers. The NRA looks at the way rivers are used, and often invests money in improving the environmental quality of British rivers.

natural In geography, this term almost always refers to something formed by nature, and not by man. See natural gas, natural hazard, natural resource, natural vegetation.

natural arch See *arch.

natural gas A *fossil fuel found in the earth's crust. Until the 1970s the UK gas supply came from coal; now most British gas is natural gas from below the North Sea. Natural gas has many advantages; it is cheap, can be stored in a concentrated, liquefied form, and is easily transported by pipeline. However, it is a *non-renewable resource.

natural hazard A hazard is an event that might be expected, but cannot be predicted. In this context, the lack of rain in the Sahara desert is not a hazard, but the rare possibility of flash flooding in the Sahara is. The most devastating natural hazards are *hurricanes, *droughts, *floods, *earthquakes, and *volcanoes. Natural hazards have their greatest effect on *less developed countries, like Bangladesh, because such countries lack the resources to cope with them.

natural increase The growth in population which comes about when the *birth rate outstrips the *death rate. It is one of the two determinants of population growth; the other is *migration. Currently, natural increase is highest in *less developed countries.

natural resource Any naturally occurring material which is used by man, such as iron ore, or virgin forest.

natural vegetation The vegetation which has developed without the influence of man.

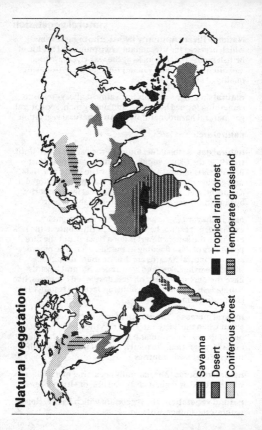

Natural vegetation

Savanna
Desert
Coniferous forest
Tropical rain forest
Temperate grassland

neap tide A tide, occurring twice a month, when the difference between high water and low water is at its least.

nearest neighbour analysis A technique used to find out if there is a pattern in the way settlements are spaced over an area. To run the test:

 (i) Measure the straight-line distance from each settlement to its nearest neighbour.

 (ii) Add the total distance of each settlement to its nearest neighbour.

 (iii) Divide this total distance by the total number of settlements to give the *observed mean* distance between nearest neighbours.

 (iv) Calculate the *observed density* of settlements using the formula:

$$\frac{\text{number of points in the study}}{\text{size of area studied}}$$

 (v) Calculate *expected mean*—the figure, if there is no pattern, using the formula:

$$\frac{1}{2\sqrt{\text{density}}}$$

 (vi) Divide the observed mean (step (iii)) by the expected mean (step (v)) to give R_n, the nearest neighbour index.

$$R_n = \frac{\text{observed mean}}{\text{expected mean}}$$

An index of 0 indicates a completely clustered pattern. 1 shows a random pattern, 2 a grid pattern, and 2.5 a triangular pattern.

neighbourhood A distinctive area within a town or city where the residents know each other by sight. **Neighbourhood amenities** are the facilities, like libraries or swimming pools, which are found locally. Neighbourhoods have tended to develop spontaneously, but *new towns in Britain have been planned with purpose-built neighbourhood units in order to give people a sense of belonging to a community.

neo-colonialism *Colonialism is the conquering and controlling of a territory by a foreign power. Most of the colonies were in what is now called the *Third World. There are very few colonies left, but the ex-colonies are still economically dependent on the old colonial powers, which tend to control the prices of the *raw materials produced by the Third World, and are the source of the *capital needed by *less developed countries.

neo-imperialism Essentially the same as neo-colonialism.

neo-Malthusianism *Malthusianism.

Network

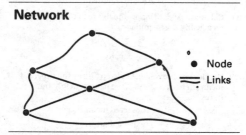

● Node

══ Links

network A system of routes which connect one settlement to another. The routes are called *links; the settlements are *nodes. ▷ accessibility, beta index, connectivity.

nevé Snow so compressed by the weight of new snow on top of it that it turns into ice.

newly industrializing country (NIC) A country, once
having had all the characteristics of a *less developed
country, which has become *industrialized. Taiwan, Singapore, Malaysia, and Hong Kong are the most successful
examples, and have industrialized by protecting their
own, growing, industries, devaluing their currencies to
make their export goods cheaper, and attracting overseas
corporations by such devices as *tax holidays and *free
trade zones.

new town A newly created town, built either on a
*greenfield site or around a settlement already in exis-
tence. New towns were created to relieve overcrowding
and congestion in cities and *conurbations; especially London, which is ringed by new towns. The aim was to launch
towns which would be self-sufficient, with their own
industries, shops, and services, with good housing and
plenty of open space. The towns were formed of *neighbourhood units, in an attempt to create new communities, with industrial development on the outskirts. They
have been criticized for lacking character, but most new
towns have been successful. The last new town in Britain
was built in 1976, but Milton Keynes, which is really a new
city, is still growing.

NIC *newly industrializing country.

nimbus A term for a cloud which will bring rain. **Nimbo-
stratus** clouds are flat, continuous cloud sheets.
▷▷cloud.

nitrate pollution Nitrates found in fertilizers are often
washed by rain-water from the fields and into streams and
rivers. There are two important effects; firstly, the nitrates
may enter supplies of drinking-water, where they may be
very harmful to health (nitrates in water have been
blamed for 'blue baby syndrome', an extremely rare
breathing difficulty in the very young). Secondly, they

increase the fertility of the water, causing *eutrophication.

nitrogen oxides Oxides of nitrogen are given off in car
exhaust fumes. They react with sunlight to form *ozone,
which is harmful to the lungs. Air with high concentrations of nitrogen oxides and hydrogen forms *photochemical smog—a frequent health hazard in car-packed cities
which are found in sunny climates, such as Los Angeles
and Mexico City.

nivation The effects of snow on a *landscape. These
include *abrasion, *frost-shattering, and *mass movements, triggered off when the snow melts.

node A point where routes meet; usually, as a result, a
more important *central place. A **nodal region** is a region
served by a central place.

nomad Someone who moves from place to place, especially a *pastoral farmer in search of grazing for his livestock. The Bedouin of North Africa are nomads, and
nomadic pastoralism is the full name given to this type
of farming. Many environmentalists have come to think
that **nomadism** is the best use of *semi-arid regions, but
as populations build up, and as governments stop people
crossing boundaries, it is a dying life-style.

nomothetic Trying to find similarities between places.
For example, *models of *urban morphology look for like-
nesses among cities. ▷ model.

non-renewable resource A *resource which, when used
up, cannot be regenerated. Oil, for example, is a non-
renewable resource because no more can be grown,
whereas wood is a *renewable resource since new trees can
be planted. Since most of the world's *energy supply
comes from non-renewable resources like *coal, *oil, and
*natural gas, attention is being turned to the production

of energy from the renewable resources of *hydroelectric, *wind, and *wave power.

normal fault A *fault where the ground has moved down the slope of the fault plane. ▷▷ fault.

North, the An alternative name for the *developed world; that is, the *more developed countries (or *advanced economies, as they are also called). The term was introduced in the *Brandt Report* (1980) to avoid any suggestion that 'more developed' indicated superiority over 'less developed'. Most of the developed world is found in the Northern Hemisphere—Europe, the *Confederation of Independent States, North America, and Japan—but the term 'North' can be misleading since Australia and New Zealand, in the Southern Hemisphere, are also part of the developed world. ▷▷ World Bank grouping, ▷ development, development indicators.

North Atlantic Drift A warm sea current flowing across the Atlantic from the Caribbean, causing temperatures along the coast of northern Europe to be higher than they would otherwise be.

North Sea Gas, North Sea Oil Reserves of *oil and *natural gas have been tapped from the bed of the North Sea since the 1970s. It became profitable to tap these reserves after the oil price shock of the early 1970s when the price of *OPEC oil quadrupled.

NRA *National Rivers Authority.

nuclear family The family unit of father, mother, and their children. ▷ extended family.

nuclear power Energy given forth from the nucleus of the atom. **Nuclear fission** is the 'splitting' of the atom; this has been the source of all our nuclear power so far, but **nuclear fusion**—the combining of atoms—should be a more effective and safer energy source. Governments have encouraged the building of **nuclear power-stations**

because they do not release *greenhouse gases, or cause
*acid rain, and they are an attractive source of energy for
regions or countries, like Brazil, without reserves of *fossil
fuels. However, there is grave concern over the costs of
nuclear power, and the possible health hazards associated
with it. In Britain, most nuclear power-stations are on the
coast, where water for cooling is readily available, and at a
distance from densely populated areas.

nucleated Clustered around a central point. **Nucleated
settlement** is concentrated in a central place. ▷▷ settlement patterns.

Nutrient cycle

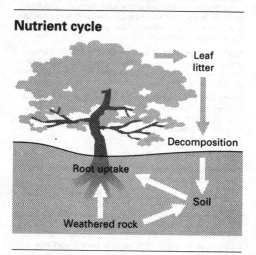

nucleus, plural **nuclei** A central part around which other things have developed. In the geography of *settlements, *central places have often developed around the nucleus of a spring, or an easily defended site.

nunatak A mountain peak which projects above an *ice sheet, and which has therefore not been exposed to *glacial erosion.

nutrient A form of nourishment. The major **plant nutrients** are nitrogen, phosphorus, and potassium, and the **nutrient cycle** is the circling of these nutrients from the soil, through the roots to a plant, and back to the soil when leaves fall, or the plant dies.

nutrition The supply of food. ▷ malnutrition, undernourishment.

O

oasis A naturally watered area in an otherwise *arid region. **Oases** are of vital importance to desert dwellers.

occlusion The final stage of many *depressions. The wedge of cold air behind a warm *front travels faster than the air in the warm sector. Eventually, it will 'catch up' on, and undercut, the warm front. The air in the warm sector is then squeezed out and lifted up. Heavy rain is associated with occlusions, which are also known as **occluded fronts**. ▷▷ front. ✍

ocean A large area of salt water. Oceans are bigger than seas, although there is no definite point at which an area

Occlusion

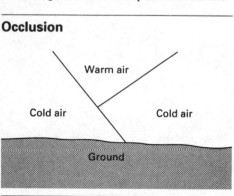

Warm air

Cold air   Cold air

Ground

of sea is considered big enough to be an ocean. Through parts of the oceans there run faster-moving streams of water, either colder or warmer than the waters around them; these are **ocean currents**, of which the *North Atlantic Drift is one example. The huge depressions holding the oceans are **ocean basins**.

ocean ridge See mid-oceanic ridge.

ocean trench A long, narrow, but very deep gorge in the *ocean floor. Ocean trenches occur at *destructive margins, where one *plate dives below another. ▷▷ plate tectonics.

offshore Slightly out to sea, but still near the land. **Offshore banks** and **offshore bars** are shallower areas of sea near the coast which may be uncovered at low *tide.

oil Also known (after *refining) as *petroleum, this is a liquid, *organic, *mineral deposit, which can be burned as an *energy source, or used as a raw material for goods ranging from plastics to drugs. An **oilfield** is an area holding underground reserves of mineral oil. Those countries which consume the most oil have to import it from countries with a surplus, and the most common method of transporting it is by **oil-tanker**. Most tankers are now very big—400 m or more in length—and can only put in at wide, deep-water harbours, known as **oil terminals**. ▷ Organization of Petroleum Exporting Countries, oil refinery.

oil price shock *Organization of Petroleum Exporting Countries.

oil refinery An industrial plant where crude *oil is split up into different fractions, such as rocket fuel, aviation fuel, petrol, and paraffin. Oil refineries need large areas of flat land and access to cooling water, and are thus often located on *estuaries.

onion weathering Also known as '**exfoliation**', this is a form of mechanical weathering which takes place where the *range of temperatures over 24 hours is wide, such as in a *desert. By day, when temperatures are high, the outermost layers of a rock expand; with the fall in temperatures at night, they contract. The strains set up by this expansion and contraction cause the outer layers of rock to split and fall off. It is believed that this process will only occur if there is some water present.

OPEC *Organization of Petroleum Exporting Countries.

opencast mining A system of mining which does not use shafts or tunnels and is therefore cheaper. The layer above the mineral is removed and the deposit beneath is taken out using earth-moving machinery. The top layer may then be replaced and landscaped. Most opencast mining is allowed on the condition that this takes place.

open space Any land which has not been built on. ▷AONB, green belt.

orbit The path taken by a planet as it moves around the sun, or by a satellite as it moves around a planet. The earth orbits the sun in a little over 365 days.

Ordnance Survey map Any map produced by the **Ordnance Survey (OS)**. The first Ordnance Survey maps were produced for the army (the term *ordnance* means guns), hence the name. The maps are produced on several *scales, the most common being 1 : 50 000 and 1 : 25 000, and all use the same *grid system, so that the same *coordinates apply for every scale. In 1989, OS map information began to be put on computer, so that customers may now order a map of the precise area they want, with the features they want, and at the scale of their choice.

ore A type of rock or sediment which contains enough of a *mineral to make it worth mining. **Ore dressing** is the partial processing of an ore, usually near the mine, so that some, but not all of the impurities are removed. It is done to cut down transport costs.

organic 1. In chemistry, containing carbon. **2.** In common use, natural, not artificial. In this context, **organic fertilizers** are of naturally occurring materials, such as manure or seaweed, and **organic farming** is farming without the use of man-made chemicals. No chemical fertilizers are used, and to keep up soil fertility, nitrogen-fixing *leguminous plants and *green manures are used.

Organization of Petroleum Exporting Countries (OPEC)
A *cartel of oil producers which attempts to control the price of petroleum. The founder members were Iran, Iraq, Kuwait, Saudi Arabia, and Venezuela; later members include Algeria, Ecuador, Gabon, Indonesia, Qatar, Nigeria, and the United Arab Emirates. In the early 1970s OPEC increased oil prices dramatically, activating an oil price shock which caused an increase in the efficiency of car engines, taxes in the USA on cars with high petrol consumption, and much greater interest in energy conservation. It was the OPEC price rises of the 1970s which made *North Sea Oil economic.

orientation Lining up a map, a person, or a surveying instrument to face North.

orogeny An earth movement which creates *mountains. This may involve *folding, *faulting, and *metamorphism.

Orogeny	Approximate date	Example
Caledonian	400 million years *BP	Scottish Highlands
Hercynian	300 million years BP	Eifel Mts., Germany
Alpine	50 million years BP	Alps

Most orogenies are associated with the movement of crustal *plates.

orographic Having to do with relief. **Orographic rainfall**, also called **relief rainfall**, forms when moisture-laden air is forced to rise when it meets high ground. The air is cooled, the water vapour in it condenses, and rain falls. This

Orographic rain

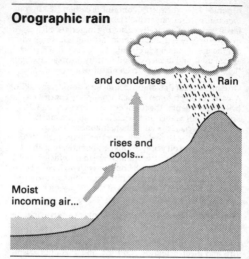

and condenses   Rain

rises and
cools...

Moist
incoming air...

explains why upland areas generally get more rain than lowlands. ▷ rain shadow.

output The end-product, or yield, of any action. If the cost of the *inputs is greater than the value of the output, the activity is *uneconomic.

outwash *Sediment carried by glacial *meltwater. An **outwash plain** is made of sands and gravels washed out by glacial meltwater and deposited beyond the glacier or ice sheet which the water came from. Usually, the coarser sediments are found nearer the *terminus of the glacier or ice sheet.

overcropping Growing crops year after year in the same ground so that the soil loses its fertility. Overcropping can lead to *soil erosion, and is said to be an indicator of *overpopulation.

overfold An overturned *fold.

overgrazing If too many animals are grazed on an area of grassland, the vegetation will be stripped, trampled, and thus destroyed. The plant roots which anchored the soil will die, and *soil erosion may result. Overgrazing is said to be a symptom of *overpopulation.

overland flow The flow of rain water over the surface. This occurs if the underlying soil or rock is saturated, or if the rainfall is so heavy that the usual process of *infiltration cannot cope.

overpopulation A region or country is said to be **overpopulated** if its *resources are not enough to keep its population at a reasonable *standard of living; in other words if its population outstrips its *carrying capacity. It is difficult to be precise about overpopulation, because there is no real agreement on minimum living standards, to show whether or not people are adequately supported, and there is no automatic link between *dense population, as in The Netherlands and Bangladesh, and poverty, which is the norm in only the second country.

over-reliance Too great a dependence on one thing. The economies of many *Third World countries are **over-reliant** on a very few export products; in 1987, for example, 99% of Nigeria's exports were of oil, and 56% of Ghana's exports were cocoa. If prices fall, or tastes change, over-reliance on a small number of industries or export goods can be very dangerous for an economy.

owner-occupier Someone who lives in, and owns, or is buying, his or her own house.

ox-bow lake A horseshoe-shaped lake once part of, but now lying alongside, a *meandering river. The lake was once part of the river, but *erosion cut through the land between the meanders, leaving the abandoned meander as a temporary lake. ▷▷ river features.

ozone A form of oxygen where three atoms of the gas are combined in one molecule, rather than two atoms, as in free oxygen. The **ozone layer** is an ozone-rich layer from 15 to 50 km above the earth's surface. Some scientists believe that the propellant gases which were used in aerosol sprays, together with *chlorofluorocarbons, are destroying the ozone layer. It is also claimed that destruction of the ozone layer (which provides protection from ultraviolet radiation) increases the risk of skin cancer.

P

Pacific rim The term given to Japan and the *newly industrializing countries, such as Taiwan and Hong Kong which are located at, or relatively near, the edge of the Pacific.

Pangaea A 'supercontinent', in existence some 200 million years ago, and consisting of all the present continents. It split up through *continental drift. ▷Gondwanaland, Laurasia.

parallel *latitude.

parasitic cone *cone.

parish At first, in Britain, an ecclesiastical area, made up of a village and a church with a clergyman in charge. A parish is now a unit of local government and does not necessarily have the same boundaries as a church parish.

pastoral Concerned with animals. **Pastoral farming** is the raising of animals such as cattle, sheep, and goats.

peasant A farmer whose activities are dominated by the family group. The family provides all the labour, and the produce is for the family as a whole. Land holdings are small, sometimes owned by the family, but often leased from a landlord. Most of the produce is consumed by the family, but, occasionally, surplus produce is sold in the open market.

peat A mass of dark brown or black plant material produced when the vegetation of a wet area is partly decomposed. Because of its high carbon content, peat may be dried and used as fuel.

pedestal rock A pillar of weak rock, capped with, and therefore protected by, a more resistant rock.

pedestrianization Closing an area, often near, or at, the city centre to motor traffic, and allowing only pedestrians to use the streets. Many cities have adopted **partial pedestrianization**, allowing buses and taxes to use the roads, but not private cars.

peninsula A piece of land jutting into the sea, and almost surrounded by it.

per annum Per year.

per capita Per head. Figures for **per capita GNP** for any country are derived by calculating *GNP and then dividing it by the numbers of nationals of that country.

perception The way people analyse and sum up the information they receive. *Human geographers are interested in people's perception of their environment because the way people *see* the world, rather than the way the world *is*, influences the way they interact with it. Many people in southern Britain believe that northern Britain is made up only of terraced houses and coal tips; in consequence, many businessmen would not dream of relocating their factories in northern Britain.

percolation The filtering of water downwards through soil and *permeable rock.

periglacial Referring to the climates and landforms of areas bordering on *ice caps and *ice sheets. Present-day periglacial areas include much of Alaska, Greenland, and Siberia, but southern Britain experienced periglacial conditions during the *Quaternary *Ice Age. The most important *geomorphological processes in periglacial regions are *freeze–thaw, *nivation, and *solifluction, and the vegetation is typical of the *tundra.

periphery Those parts of a region, country, or even the world, which are isolated, and away from areas of thriving economic development, that is, away from the *cores. ▷core–periphery model.

permafrost Areas of rock and soil where temperatures have been below freezing-point for at least two years. Permafrost lies below the surface layer of the ground, which will thaw in summer. It is difficult to build in permafrost areas because the ground is like iron, and when buildings are occupied, the heat they give off can melt the permafrost, causing the buildings to subside.

permanent pasture Grassland constantly used for the grazing of *livestock. Most areas of permanent pasture are found in areas of ample rainfall (over 800 mm per annum), where temperatures are mild.

permeable Allowing water to pass through. Rivers rarely flow over permeable rocks such as chalk or limestone (but see dry valley).

pH A measurement of the acidity of a substance. A pH of 1 to 6 is acid, 7 is neutral, and 8 to 12 are alkaline.

photochemical smog A *smog formed when oxides of nitrogen, given off in car-exhaust fumes, react with sunlight to form *ozone, which is harmful to the lungs. The ozone also reacts with more nitrogen oxides to make more photochemical smog, in a dangerous feedback loop. Furthermore, the hydrocarbons emitted from the burning of *fossil fuels can also contribute to the smog. Photochemical smog is a frequent health hazard in car-packed cities which are found in sunny climates, such as Los Angeles and Mexico City.

photosynthesis The manufacture of carbohydrates by green plants, using carbon dioxide from the air, and energy from the sun. Oxygen is given off in the process.

Were it not for photosynthesis, all oxygen-breathing species on earth would now be extinct.

physical environment The *natural, as opposed to the man-made, environment.

physical geography That section of *geography which deals with the *natural features of the earth. Physical geography includes the study of *weather and *climates, soils, *ecosystems, *hydrology, and *geomorphology.

physical quality of life A measure of living standards which takes into account *infant mortality, *life expectancy, and basic *literacy.

physical weathering *mechanical weathering.

pie chart A way of showing data in percentage or proportional form by dividing a circle into segments. To draw a pie chart:

(i) Convert all your numbers into percentages of the total. Put them in rank order, largest first.

Pie chart

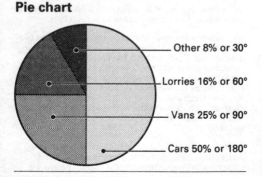

Other 8% or 30°

Lorries 16% or 60°

Vans 25% or 90°

Cars 50% or 180°

(ii) Since there are 360˚ in a circle, each percentage point will be represented by 3.6˚. Thus, multiply each percentage by 3.6˚. The result of this sum will give you the angle at the centre of each segment in degrees. ✍

piedmont Describing a feature found at the foot of mountains. In the USA, **the Piedmont** is a zone at the foot of the Appalachian Mountains.

plain A lowland. ▷coastal plain.

planning authority The *administrative body which studies **planning applications** for new development. This authority may be a district council, city council, or county council.

planning permission Almost all new development must be studied by the local authority before it is begun, to check that it will not conflict with the character of the area it is to be situated in. Planning permission is given if the development is approved. In many cases, local authorities set up **planning restrictions**; these are blocks to certain types of development, such as the location of a new factory in a *residential area.

plant 1. In a system, the buildings, machinery, and land into which *inputs are made and from which *outputs emerge. 2. In industrial geography, an individual factory producing power or manufactured goods.

plantation A large farm, generally under a monoculture, for the production of tropical and subtropical crops. The holdings are big, and the labour force is large. The first stage of processing often takes place on site. Plantations usually produce tree and bush crops and were often developed by *colonial powers. With independence, many *Third World countries have nationalized their plantations or redistributed the land. **Plantation agriculture** is typical of the Third World.

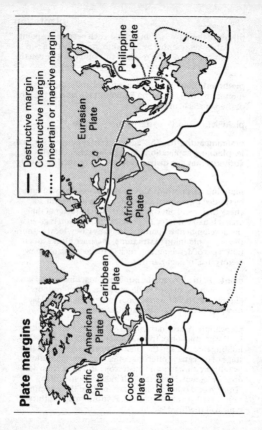

Plate margins

Plate margins

Destructive margin
Constructive margin
Uncertain or inactive margin

Pacific Plate
American Plate
Caribbean Plate
Cocos Plate
Nazca Plate

Eurasian Plate
African Plate
Philippine Plate

plate A rigid segment of the earth's crust which can 'float' across the heavier, semi-molten rock below. The plates making up the continents—**continental plates**—are less dense but thicker than those making up the oceans—the **oceanic plates**. A **plate boundary**, or **plate margin** is the edge of a plate, and **plate tectonics** is the name given to the movements of the plates. Fundamentally, plates move because *magma wells up at *constructive plate margins, as in the mid-Atlantic. It is here that new plate material is formed, and this new material pushes the plate aside. At *destructive margins, plates are forced together. The denser plate dives below the other, as at the margin of the Pacific and Eurasian plates. Destructive margins are associated with *earthquakes, *volcanoes, and *fold mountains.   ✍🏻

plateau A large, relatively flat, upland area.

plucking The removal of loose bedrock as it is pulled away by moving glacier ice. Since ice is not very strong, plucking generally occurs only when the rock is already jointed and/or weathered.

plug A mass of solidified lava in the neck of a *volcano. Sometimes, as in Ship Rock, USA, the surrounding volcano is eroded away, leaving the more resistant rock standing out as a huge 'spike'.

plunge pool A pool at the base of a waterfall, often undercutting the sheer rock face. Plunge pools form as a result of *hydraulic action and *chemical erosion.   ✍🏻

pluralism This term may be used to describe any set-up where no particular political, cultural, or *ethnic group dominates any others.

plural society A society made up of a number of distinct groupings, which may be of race, religion, or languages. Classic examples are given below:

Type of plural society	Example
Race	Republic of South Africa
Religion	Bosnia-Hercegovina
Language	Belgium

As you can see from the first two examples, many plural societies can become so badly divided that violence results.

plutonic rock An *igneous rock which has cooled and crystallized slowly, deep below the surface of the earth.

polder A flat area of land which has been reclaimed from the sea. The term comes from The Netherlands, where large areas have been ringed by sea-walls, drained of water, cleansed of salt, and used for farming, thereby increasing the area of the country by one-fifth.

Plunge pool

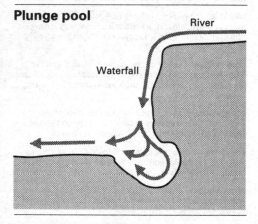

political asylum The permission given to a *migrant to stay in a foreign country because he or she is threatened with persecution, brought about solely because of the asylum-seeker's political beliefs, in the home country.

pollution An unwelcome change in the physical, chemical, or biological characteristics of the *natural environment. Although there are some natural *pollutants such as volcanoes, pollution generally occurs because of human activity. Biodegradable pollutants, like sewage, cause no permanent damage if they are properly dealt with, but non-biodegradable pollutants, such as lead, may get into the *food chain. Other forms of environmental pollution include noise and the release of heat into waterways, which may damage aquatic life. Present-day problems of pollution include *acid rain and *global warming.

pools and riffles Many rivers show a repeated pattern of deeper stretches—pools—and shallower sections—riffles—along their straighter courses. Some experts think that pools and riffles are the first stage in the development of *meanders.

population The number of people living in a given region, such as a city, a county, or a country. **Population density** is the average number of people in a given area, usually a square kilometre. *Dense population is not necessarily the same as *overpopulation; Britain and Sri Lanka have similar crude densities (about 220 per km^2), but very different living standards. ▷ population distribution.

population change Any change in the numbers or *distribution of a population. Population change may occur because of alterations in the *birth and/or *death rates, or because of *migration. ▷ demographic transition model.

population control The attempt to limit the growth of population through the use of contraception and by government 'persuasion'. The most successful example of population control is that of China. By a system of fines and/or demotions for parents with families larger than one child, raising the age of marriage, and by forced sterilizations and abortions, China has managed to slow down the rate of population growth, but the policy has not been as effective as was hoped.

population distribution The way in which population is spread out over an area, region, nation, continent, or the world. Certain factors encourage dense populations—over 200 per km²: *temperate climates, good soils, an abundant supply of water, and thriving *industries. By comparison *sparsely populated regions—under 10 per km² may have extremely hot or cold climates, low annual rainfall (under 400 mm), difficult vegetation, or be distant from *core areas of development.

population explosion The term given to the extremely rapid growth in world population numbers in the last 50 years. This growth has been due mainly to improved sanitation and better medical care. World population is now likely to double every 35–45 years, and if this rate of growth is sustained, there will be severe problems of *overpopulation in the next century. The problem is more acute in the *Third World because a large proportion of the population there is very young.

population pyramid See age–sex pyramid.

population structure The make-up of a population by age and by sex. This is usually illustrated by *age–sex pyramids. Generally speaking, more boys are born than girls. In the past, the sexes balanced out because *infant mortality rates were higher for boys, but with modern medicine, this is no longer the case.

porous rock A rock containing many tiny air spaces, or holes; chalk is an example. Most porous rocks are *permeable.

port A place where ships can anchor to load and unload cargo. Most ports are based on naturally occurring *harbours which have then been enlarged and protected by building sea-walls; some, like Tema, in Ghana, are entirely artificial.

post-industrial country A country which is centred on *information technology, where *services are the dominant form of industry, and with a large professional and technical class. It is not clear whether a true post-industrial society has yet emerged.

pothole A more or less circular hole in the bedrock of a river. The hole gets larger because pebbles trapped inside it scrape away the bedrock as the water swirls them round.

power *energy.

PQL *physical quality of life.

prairie An extensive area of flat, naturally occurring grassland, such as the **Prairies** of Canada. Recently, the term has been used to describe fairly flat *arable land with large fields and no hedges between them; since the removal of hedges, much of East Anglia has been called a 'prairie'.

precipitation Any form of water falling on to the earth's surface from the *atmosphere. The main categories are dew, fog, frost, hail, mist, rain, sleet, and snow.

pre-industrial society A society with mostly *cottage industries, and with the majority of its population dependent on agriculture.

pressure The weight of the atmosphere as it presses down on to the earth's surface. **Low pressure** (under 996 *mb) is generally caused by rising air—for example when it is warmed. **High pressure** is usually the result of an influx of cold, heavy air, or of air being forced downwards from high in the atmosphere. A **pressure belt** is a zone of high or low pressure. ▷▷ general circulation of the atmosphere.

prevailing wind The wind direction which occurs most often at any given place. ▷ wind belt. Remember that winds are called after the direction they blow *from*, and not *to*. ▷▷ general circulation of the atmosphere.

primary First. **Primary data**, for example, is knowledge in its first state, before it has been analysed or processed. ▷ primary industry.

primary industry Any industry concerned with the extraction or production of *raw materials, such as mining, fishing, forestry, or agriculture. That part of a country's economy which is involved with primary industry is known as the **primary sector**.

primate city A city which is very much larger than any other in a country. It is not only more important than any other in terms of size; it is also dominant politically and economically. London, for example, is more than six times larger than Birmingham, the second city in the UK. Most primate cities are found in *less developed countries. **Primacy** is the condition of being primate. ▷ hierarchy.

process 1. (noun) The way in which something is brought about. Thus, the process of *gentrification can bring about *urban renewal, and the process of *freeze–thaw can form *scree. 2. (verb) To produce a partly or fully-finished product from *raw materials.

projection 1. A particular method of showing the spherical surface of the earth as a flat map. See *map for a description of the different qualities of different map projections. 2. An estimate of a future development based on past trends. The illustration shows three projections which have been made of total world population for the year AD 2000. ✍

Projection

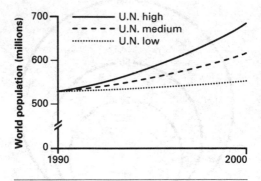

pro-natalist policy Government policy designed to bring about a rise in the *birth rate. Up until 1990, the Romanian government tried to keep birth rates high by banning both *contraception and abortion.

proportional circle A way of showing data, such as the size of British cities, by drawing a circle in proportion to the statistics. To draw proportional circles:

(i) It is the *area* of the circle that should be in proportion. Since the area of a circle = πr^2, calculate the correct *radius* (r) for each statistic by calculating its square root.

(ii) When you have calculated the correct values for the radii, you might have to use a scale if the answers are too big or too small for your map. Halving or doubling the values usually works.

Proportional circles

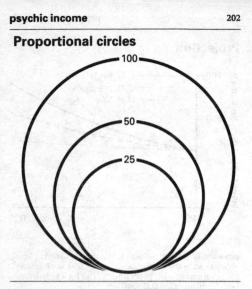

psychic income Something gained which cannot be measured in cash terms. For example, someone moving from London to the same job, at the same salary, but in the Lake District, would have the psychic income of clean air and mountain scenery.

pull factor Any factor which tempts people to migrate *towards* another location. In a questionnaire directed to Ghanaians who had moved to Accra, the following pull factors were given (in order of importance):

1. Job prospects in the city.
2. Better educational facilities.

3. Gas, piped water, and electricity.
4. Freedom from restrictive ways of life (especially for women).
5. Entertainment facilities.

▷ push factor, urbanization, migration.

pulse Any edible seed of a *leguminous plant, such as peas or beans. Pulses are high in protein and 'fix' nitrogen from the air into their roots, thus naturally improving the soil's fertility.

pumped storage scheme Electricity cannot be stored in large quantities, so when demand is low, at night, excess power can be used to pump water uphill from a lower to a higher reservoir. At peak-demand times, the water is allowed to flow back downwards, passing through generators as it goes, and thus producing *HEP. Pumped storage schemes actually use more energy than they make, but do use up surplus electricity.

push factor Any factor which tempts people to migrate *away from* another location. Examples include lack of land, lack of jobs, war, and *natural hazards, such as *drought.

pyramidal peak A sharp, pointed, mountain summit found in regions of *glacial erosion, and formed when three or more *corries, back to back, eat into the original mountain top.

pyroclast A fragment of solidified lava, thrown out during a *volcanic eruption.

Q

quadrat A metal frame, usually square in shape, and often sub-divided into 10 smaller squares. It is used in *sampling.

quarrying 1. The removal of rock or stone from any large excavation. 2. The preferred term for *plucking.

quartz The mineral silicon dioxide, often found in crystal form in *sedimentary or *metamorphic rocks, or as a vein running through a rock.

Quaternary The most recent period of geological time, which began about 2 million years ago. It was during the Quaternary that Britain experienced a major *ice age.

quaternary industry The sale of advice and information; examples include teaching and investment consultancies. That part of a country's economy which is involved with quaternary industry is known as the **quaternary sector**.

quay A dock side, where ships can load and unload.

quota A numerical limit. Many countries use a quota system to limit immigration; in the most famous example, the USA had a fixed total limit of immigrants, with the precise numbers allowed in from each country in proportions to the numbers from each country already resident in the United States. Quotas may also be used to restrict the number of imports allowed into a country. This can be done to protect industries or to improve the *balance of trade.

R

racial tension Difficulties between members of different *ethnic groups. Racial tensions are not unusual in *plural, or multicultural, societies, and often take the form of anti-immigrant feeling.

rain A type of *precipitation consisting of water droplets larger than 1 mm in diameter. (Smaller droplets will 'float' in the air as mist or fog.) Rainfall totals are measured with a **rain gauge**; a wide-mouthed funnel leading into a cylinder. Rain gauges are checked daily, and the totals are usually recorded in millimetres. If the amount of water in the gauge is too small to be measured, it is recorded as **trace rain**. ▷convection rain, frontal rain, relief rain.

rain shadow An area of relatively low rainfall on the *lee (sheltered) side of an *upland. The incoming air has been forced to rise over the highland, causing rain to fall on the windward side, and thus lowering the amount of water content in the air as it flows down the lee side.

range In descriptions of climates, the difference between the highest and lowest temperatures in a day (**diurnal range**) or over a year (**annual range**).

range of a good or service The maximum distance a person will travel to buy a given good or service. For example, a customer would expect to travel much further to buy an Old Master drawing than to buy a pint of milk.

rank Degree of importance. *Spearman's rank test puts two sets of data in **rank order** to see if there is any relationship between them.

Rank-size rule

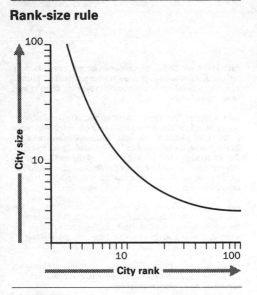

rank-size rule Settlements in a country may be *ranked in order of their size. The 'rule' states that if the population of a town is multiplied by its rank, the sum will equal the population of the highest ranked city. In other words, the population of a town ranked n will be $1/n$th of the size of the largest city. This 'rule' rarely works in practice! ✍

rapids Areas of very unsettled water across a river, which may make river transport impossible. Unlike waterfalls, rapids are the result of a continuous and relatively gentle slope, rather than a sudden vertical drop.

raw material Anything which can be *processed to make a finished or partly finished, product. In *industrial location theory, raw materials are an important *locational factor in *heavy industry.

in real terms An expression used by economists when they want to compare monetary values, like prices or wages, at a time when the value of money is changing. If I earn twice as much as I did ten years ago, but the price of everything I buy has doubled, or the value of my money has halved, I am no better off in real terms. In the same way, economists talk of **real prices**; if it takes me three times as long to earn the money for a good as it did a year ago, its real price—the 'price' I pay through my labour—has risen, even though the numbers on the price ticket are just the same.

recreation Any leisure activity lasting less than twenty-four hours.

recycling Re-using resources in an effort to make the most of their value, cut down on waste, and lessen environmental disturbance. In Britain, the 1980s saw an increase in recycling, especially of glass and paper. The recycling of scrap metal is a major source of metal in refineries from Ghana to The Netherlands.

redevelopment Demolishing old buildings and creating new ones on the same site. Redevelopment can solve existing problems of *congestion and poor housing, but for residential areas in particular, it can destroy communities, and create urban wastelands until the new building takes place. Many British city centres have been redeveloped. The old city centres grew up before cars were invented, and when the population of the city was smaller, so that, today, many old city centres are too cramped. Redevelopment in the city centre has brought about shopping centres and *pedestrianization.

redlining Banks and building societies often put a 'red line' on maps of the city to mark out less prosperous areas where they are unwilling to lend money for house purchase or home improvements, thus contributing to the downward spiralling of poorer areas.

refinery A *processing plant designed to purify, that is, **refine**, a resource, especially *crude oil. Most **oil refineries** are located in the countries which consume most oil, and because of the size of modern oil-tankers, are often located on deep-water *harbours.

regeneration Renewal, revival. The term can apply to a patch of rain forest, cleared for agriculture but then left to **regenerate**, or to a declining area of a city which is regenerated by *gentrification or *urban renewal.

region Any part of the earth's surface with characteristics which mark it off as being different from the areas around it. A **natural region**, such as Amazonia, developed without the influence of man; examples of human regions include *hinterlands and urban fields as well as areas like the Midlands.

regional To do with a region. **Regional imbalance**, or **regional inequality** is a marked difference in living standards between different regions within a nation. This could show up as variations in unemployment or per capita income in *developed countries or in life expectancy and infant mortality rates in *less developed countries. **Regional development plans** are set up in an attempt to lessen these differences. ▷ development area.

rejuvenation The revitalizing of a process which has begun to run down. In geography, this word is generally applied to streams and rivers which regain their energy when the land they flow over rises through earth move-

Rejuvenation

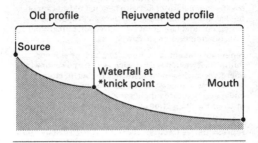

Old profile   Rejuvenated profile

Source

Waterfall at
*knick point   Mouth

ments, or when the sea-level falls. Rejuvenation causes the
river to erode more powerfully, and this downcutting
starts at the mouth and works its way upstream. Waterfalls often occur at the landward end of the rejuvenated
section. ▷knick point.   ✍

relationship A connection, or link. Geographers are interested, for example, in the links between the *physical
world and man's activities, or between poverty and *birth
rates. It is possible to investigate the link, or *correlation
between two features, known as *variables, by drawing
*scatter graphs or by using a statistical test, the easiest of
which—*Spearman's rank test—is explained in this book.

relative humidity A measurement of the moisture content of the air. It is calculated as the ratio between the
amount of water vapour in a given quantity of air and the
maximum amount that air *could* carry at the same temperature. Relative humidity is expressed as a percentage; saturated air has a relative humidity of 100%.

relief The shape of the earth's surface.

relief rain Rain which falls when moist air is forced to rise over an upland area. As the moist air rises, it cools, because temperatures fall with height. Cold air cannot hold as much water vapour, so the water vapour *condenses out, and falls as rain. ▷ convection rain, frontal rain, orographic, rain shadow.

renewable resource A *resource which *either* is not diminished when it is used, such as water power or wind energy, *or* can be grown again, like timber, or crops. This second type of renewable resource can be used without endangering future supplies as long as this use does not outstrip the production of new resources, as in fishing. ▷ sustainable development.

representative fraction The ratio between distance on a map and distance on the ground: the scale. If 1 cm on a map symbolizes 50 000 cm (0.5 km) on the ground, the representative fraction is 1 : 50 000.

reservoir A man-made lake, used to store water which is later supplied to homes and industry. It may also be used for leisure activities, or to make *hydroelectric power. ▷ multi-purpose river project, multiple land use.

residential To do with housing; suburbs are primarily residential areas.

resistant rock A hard rock, which is not easily *eroded, for example, granite. ▷ differential erosion, headland, scarp, yardang, zeuge.

resource Things which people can use. These may be **natural resources**—*ores, water, soil, *natural vegetation, or even climate; or **human resources**—labour, skills, finance, capital, and technology. ▷ renewable resource, non-renewable resource.

restoration *environmental restoration.

retail To do with shops. The best retail locations were once in the *CBD; increasingly, the best retail locations are on out-of-town sites.

reverse(d) fault A *fault where the line of the fault (the fault plane) slopes towards the beds which have moved upwards. ▷▷ fault.

ria An inlet of the sea, formed when a river valley flooded because of a rise in sea-level.

ribbon development A built-up area along a main road running outwards from the city centre.

ribbon lake A long, narrow lake, situated in a *glacial trough.

Richter scale A scale measuring the magnitude of earthquakes, and ranging from 0 to 10. On this scale a value of 2 can just be felt as a tremor. Damage to buildings occurs for values of over 6, and the largest shock ever recorded had a magnitude of 8.9. The Richter scale is a logarithmic scale, so that 4 on the scale is very much more than double the strength of 2.

ridge A long, narrow, steep-sided upland. **Ridge and vale**, or **ridge and valley** country is a series of almost parallel ridges, separated by narrow valleys. The ridges are often of more resistant rock than the valleys.

rift valley A long valley which has sunk down between roughly parallel *faults. Examples include the East African rift valley and the Rhine rift valley. **Rifting** is often associated with *plate movements. ▷▷ fault.

river A course of water, larger than a stream (but there is no agreed width at which a stream becomes a river). A **river course** is the path taken by a river; a river with all its tributaries is a **river system**, and the area drained by a river system is a **river basin**. ▷ stream order.

Ria

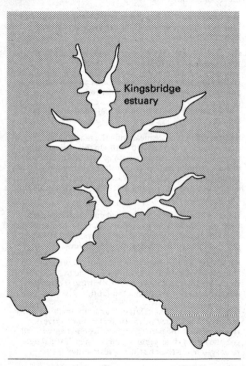

Kingsbridge estuary

river cliff A *bluff at the outside bend of a meander, often made deeper when the meander is *incised. ▷▷ river features.

river features These include *bluffs, *braided channels, *flood plain *incised meanders, *interlocking spurs, *meanders, *ox-bow lakes, *river cliffs, *river terraces, *slip-off slopes.   ✎

river management Controlling the flow of a river to lessen the risk of flooding; methods include the use of dams, sluices, and locks. The river may also be managed to produce *hydroelectric power, and irrigation water. Leisure activities may be encouraged, and efforts can be made to cut the flow of *effluents into the river and increase the supply of oxygen in the water. ▷ multi-purpose river project.

river terrace A low, bench-like 'step' running along a valley side, roughly parallel with the valley walls. Most terraces form when the power of the river to erode increases, so that it cuts through its *floodplain.

roche moutonnée A rock shaped by two different processes of *glacial erosion. Its up-side and centre have been polished by *abrasion; its down-side is rugged and steep, and has been *quarried. Roches moutonnées may be over 100 m in height and up to 1 km in length, but they are usually much smaller. ▷▷ glacial erosion.

rock A naturally formed, more or less solid section of the earth's *crust. Rocks are classified by the way they were formed—*igneous, *metamorphic, or *sedimentary; by their composition, for example, *limestone; or by the *geological time in which they were laid down.

rock creep The gradual movement downslope of rock fragments (*scree). It is a form of *mass movement.

rock dam A simple barrier, made of rocks, laid across a *gully to slow down the speed of water, so that it soaks

River features

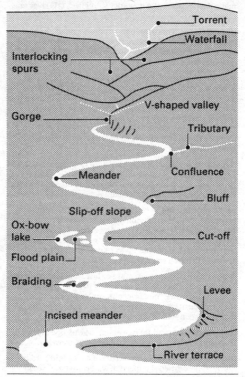

into the ground rather than eroding the soil and running away. It is a simple piece of *intermediate technology, used in *arid lands.

rotation Planting a sequence of crops, in order to preserve the fertility of the soil. Thus, if a crop which takes a lot out of the soil, such as maize, is planted, it can be followed next year by a *leguminous crop, or *green manure, to put nitrogen back into the soil. Rotation also guards against the build-up of disease and pests in the soil.

rough grazing Natural, or semi-natural grassland, usually unfenced, used as *grazing land. Most of the rough grazing in Britain is in upland areas.

route A journey line, usually a road, railway track, or waterway. A **route centre** is a place where several routes converge; London, for example, is the major route centre of the UK. Route centres are highly *accessible, and often become centres of trade and industry. ▷ node, edge.

runoff The movement of rain-water over the ground. Runoff occurs when the rainfall is very heavy so that the rocks and soil cannot absorb any more water. ▷▷ hydrological cycle.

rural To do with the countryside. In practice, it is often difficult to distinguish truly rural areas because town merges into countryside throughout the *rural–urban fringe and because many rural inhabitants work in cities, so that a place which *looks* rural may not actually have most of its population working in rural occupations.

rural depopulation Also known as **rural–urban migration**, this is the fall in population of rural areas, whether by migration, or by a sharp drop in birth rates as young people move away. It has been blamed on the mechanization of agriculture, which led to rural unemployment. One extreme example in Britain was on the island of St Kilda, where the last few, elderly, inhabitants were evacuated in 1930. No one lives there now. ▷ migration, pull factor, push factor.

rural–urban fringe The zone where the town or city blends into countryside. Many *urban areas have no clear-cut boundary; instead, the houses become more scattered, there are stables, filling stations, garden centres, and pick-your-own farms, and it is some while before the surroundings are fully *rural.

Sahel A *semi-arid zone of Africa, lying between the Sahara Desert and the *savanna, and stretching from Senegal to the Sudan. It suffers frequent droughts because of the unreliability of the rain-bearing *Inter Tropical Convergence Zone—the last very severe drought was in 1984—and therefore famine is often a threat.

salination, salinization The build-up of salts at or near the surface of a soil. In dry climates, surface water evaporates rapidly. This brings the soil moisture to the surface, together with the salts dissolved in it. The water then evaporates, leaving behind a crust of salts on the surface. Badly managed irrigation in *arid lands can cause salinization; and, in coastal districts, salinization can occur when sea-water seeps into the soil after too much groundwater has been pumped out.

saline Salty.

Saltation

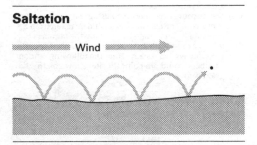

saltation The 'bouncing' of material from and along a river bed or a land surface. ✍

salt marsh A *saline *wetland. Salt marshes develop around *estuaries and *spits, and the vegetation is especially adapted to the salt water.

sample A portion of the total which is taken to represent the whole. Opinion surveys, for example, sample about 1000 people and from this predict the opinions of the whole population; and ecologists sample several tiny areas, using *quadrats, to make assumptions about the ecology of a large area. **Sampling** is taking measurements of a portion of a feature you are studying, such as the number of daisies in a small part of a lawn, in order to estimate the total number of daisies over the whole lawn. You can make a **systematic sample** using a quadrat, and selecting sample points that are equally spaced over the area under investigation.

Alternatively, you can take a **random sample** by placing your quadrats at random intervals. This is how to go about it:

(i) Put a tape along the longest side of your area.

(ii) Put a second measuring tape at right angles to the first, and at one end. These tapes will serves as the axes of your survey area.

(iii) Locate your survey points by using coordinates from these axes. The coordinates should be taken from a table of random numbers. Use only the numbers which would apply to your tape, and work through the table systematically. Thus, the following random numbers would pin-point the sites shown on the diagram below:

'x' axis	'y' axis
4260	2360
2653	1807
3931	6057
0016	4126
1043	3237

✍

Sample (1)

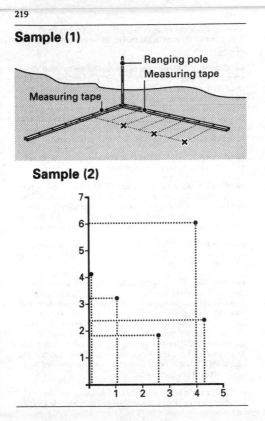

Sample (2)

sand Particles of rock with diameters ranging from 0.06 mm to 2.00 mm in diameter. Most sands are formed of quartz.

sand-dune A hill or ridge of sand built up by wind *deposition. Once a dune is formed, sand will settle on it rather than on bare surfaces. This is because the friction of the sandy surface is enough to slow down the wind, which then sheds some of its *load. In this way, the dune gets larger. A characteristic feature of sand-dunes is that they are constantly moving and changing as a result of wind action. ▷ barchan, seif dune, ▷▷ desert features.

sandstone A *sedimentary rock made up of compacted grains of sand, cemented together.

satellite image A picture taken from a man-made satellite, carrying the cameras known as 'remote sensors'. The information picked up by the sensors has to be put into visual form by computers, because the sensors can pick up wavelengths, like infra-red light, which we cannot see.

satellite town A *new town or *dormitory town developed to take population relocated after *slum clearance in a nearby *urban area.

savanna Tropical grassland, flanking each side of the *tropical rain forests of Africa and South America. The grass is coarse, and the scattered trees are modified to cut down the loss of water loss via *transpiration; they have small flat leaves and are often thorny. The savanna has no clear boundaries; there is a gradual change from tall grasses with scattered trees, to grassy woodland, and then to rain forest. Savanna vegetation is probably not *natural vegetation, but has been brought about by repeated burning. ▷▷ natural vegetation.

scale The ratio between an actual distance, on the ground, and the distance on a map of that area. Scales can be shown by *representative fractions, or by **scale diagrams**. ▷▷ linear scale.

scarp, scarp slope A steep slope. **Scarp-foot springs** emerge at the foot of scarps. ▷▷ cuesta.

scatter diagram or **graph** A way of showing data to see if there is any *correlation between two sets of *variables. To draw a scatter diagram:

(i) Using graph paper, draw two axes, at right angles to each other.

(ii) Decide on suitable scales for your two variables. Number and label the axes.

(iii) Plot each point, using each pair of variables as *coordinates.

(iv) Draw a *best-fit line through the points.

(v) If the best-fit line seems to be diagonal, a *correlation is implied.

scenic To do with scenery, usually scenery of outstanding natural beauty. ▷ Area of Outstanding Natural Beauty.

science park An industrial development set up close to a university or research institute, in order for industry to benefit from research discoveries, and for academic researchers to learn about business methods. ▷ high-tech.

scree Shattered rock fragments which fall from rock faces and mountain summits, and accumulate at the foot of the slope. ▷▷ mass movement.

scrub Low, often thick, shrubby vegetation, often forming on poor soils or when a forest *regenerates itself when land is no longer cultivated.

sea breeze Land heats more rapidly than water. In coastal districts, this means that on sunny days, the land is warmer than the sea. The air above the land is warmed, and rises. Air from the sea streams in to replace the air above the land, and this is a sea breeze. Sea breezes often bring cooler conditions in the afternoon to areas with hot, humid climates. ▷ land breeze.

sea-floor spreading The creation of new *crust as *magma rises up at a *plate margin. The magma pushes the plates apart, creating new oceanic crust and pushing away the far end of the plate.

sea-level The average level of the sea surface from which all contour heights are taken.

seasonal Occurring, often in a regular pattern, at a particular season in the year.

secondary industry The making of finished products from *raw materials; that is, manufacturing. That part of the economy concerned with manufacturing is known as the **secondary sector**.

sector model Also known as the Hoyt model, this is a *model of *urban structure. Housing areas in a city are said to develop in sections along routes outwards from the *CBD, with high-quality located very often on higher ground. Industrial sectors develop along canals and railways, away from high-quality housing.

sedentary agriculture Any farming system where the farmer is settled in one spot. Compare with *nomadic and *shifting agriculture, and *transhumance.

sediment Material which has separated and settled out from the force which originally carried it, whether wind, water, or ice. From this term come the words **sedimentary** and **sedimentary rock**; made up of sediments. ▷ load.

seif dune A long, narrow *sand-dune, formed when two *prevailing winds alternate, either daily or seasonally. ▷▷ desert features.

seismic To do with *earthquakes. A **seismograph** is an instrument used to record earthquake activity, and **seismology** is the study of earthquakes.

seismic gap theory *Earthquakes occur along *fault lines and *plate margins. If the distribution of earthquakes is plotted along a given fault, it is possible to identify places where there has been very little earthquake activity: the seismic 'gaps'. Some geologists believe that these places are overdue for an earthquake. Acting on this belief, American geologists predicted in the 1980s that Parkfield was the most likely spot for the next Californian earthquake. By 1992 they had given up waiting and moved their *seismographs out!

selva The *tropical rain forest of Latin America.

semi Half, partly. From this come **semi-arid**: less dry than a *desert, but with rainfall below 500 mm a year; and **semi-desert**: not true desert, a semi-arid area.

service industry Any economic activities (including wholesaling, transport, and retailing) concerned with the distribution and consumption of goods and services together with administration, and, possibly, the provision of information, although this last category can be called *quaternary industry. Any central place providing services may be called a **service centre**, and those parts of the economy concerned with service industries make up the **service sector**.

settlement In human geography, any form of human habitation from a single house to the largest city. A **settlement hierarchy** is a division of settlements into ranks, usually according to the size of the population. In theory, the greater the rank of a settlement, the more goods and services it provides.

settlement pattern The nature of the distribution of settlements. Common settlement patterns are *nucleated, *linear, and *dispersed. *Nearest neighbour analysis can be used to test for any regularities in settlement patterns. ✍

shading map *choropleth.

Settlement pattern

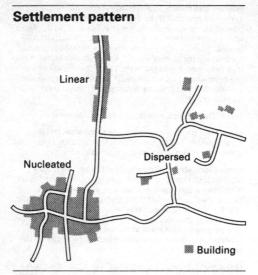

shale A soft, fine-grained *sedimentary rock formed when layers of clay are compressed by the weight of overlying rocks.

shanty town An area of makeshift housing, generally at the edge of a *Third World city. Shanty towns grow because demand for cheap housing outstrips supply, and houses are made from any available cheap materials such as packing-cases, metal cans, plywood, and cardboard. Sanitation is grossly inadequate, electricity and gas may not be available, and roads are not metalled. Many city authorities try to bulldoze the shanty towns, but some, as in Lima, Peru, are trying to upgrade the settlements, with the co-operation of the inhabitants. ▷ bastee, bidonville, favela.

share-cropping A type of *land tenure; here the tenant pays rent in the form of a proportion of the crops. There is little reason for the tenant to grow more crops because he then pays more rent.

shield The very old, rigid core of relatively stable rocks within a continent. Examples include the Canadian Shield.

shifting cultivation In this agricultural system, a patch of land is cleared, crops are grown, and the patch is then deserted until the soil regains its fertility. The farmers move house, to be near a new site. *Bush fallowing is shifting cultivation but involves no change of residence, grows crops for longer, and uses a shorter fallow. ▷ slash and burn.

shopping centre, shopping mall A covered area, often on more than one level, containing a large number of shops. Shopping centres are usually in city centres and, in Britain close to public transport. Shopping malls are often at the edge of the city, where parking is easy, and can take away business from city centre shops; for example, out-of-town malls have 'killed' most of the shops in central Los Angeles.

sial The rocks of the continental *crust, dominated by minerals rich in silica and aluminium.

sierra The Spanish term for a *mountain range.

silage Green crops, such as grass and clover, which have been compressed, fermented, and stored in a **silo**, or air-tight tower, for use as animal fodder.

silicon chip The microchip which is the basic component of most *electronic goods. From this comes **Silicon Glen**

and **Silicon Fen**—areas around Glenrothes (Central Scotland) and Cambridge respectively where many electronics firms are based.

sill An *intrusion of *igneous rock which has spread along *bedding planes in a nearly horizontal sheet. This level sheet may be up to 300 m in thickness. ▷▷ intrusion.

silt A fine-grained soil, often laid down by rivers in flood.

sima The rocks of the lower continental *crust and the oceanic crust, dominated by minerals rich in silica and magnesium.

Single European Market The abandonment of most *customs duties within the *European Community in order to encourage *trade, which came into effect in January 1993.

sink hole A roughly circular depression in a limestone area into which one or more streams drain.

site The position of a settlement in physical, local terms. For example, Durham Cathedral is sited inside an *incised meander. ▷ situation.

Site of Special Scientific Interest (SSSI) A site in the UK which is of particular importance because of its *geology, *relief, or *ecology. Planning permission for the development of the SSSI is granted only after consultation with the Nature Conservancy Council.

situation The location of a settlement in relation to other settlements, or within a *region.

six-figure grid reference *grid reference.

sketch map A free-hand map, illustrating some of the key features in a region. ✍

slash and burn The basic technique of clearing land for *shifting cultivation. The cleared vegetation is burned on-site; this returns the nutrients in the plants to the soil.

Sketch map

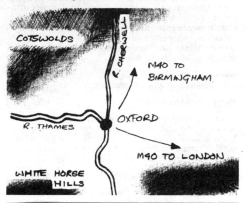

slate A weak *sedimentary rock, formed by the compression of *shales, and easily split along its thin *bedding planes. Because of this quality, slate has been a very important roofing material. When artificial slates were developed, towns like Blaenau Ffestiniog in North Wales experienced severe unemployment.

sleet A mixture of rain and snow, or rain and hail.

slides, slips Two forms of *mass movement.

slip-off slope The relatively gentle slope at the inner edge of a *meander. ▷▷ river features.

slum An area of poor housing, often characterized by multi-occupance and overcrowding. Schools are poor, buildings are deteriorating, and although items sold in local shops are relatively expensive many residents cannot afford the transport to shop more cheaply elsewhere. Slums often have a high proportion of drug abusers, alcoholics, crime, and vandalism. After the Second World War, **slum clearance schemes** were very common, and the inhabitants were often rehoused in new estates at the edge of the city, like Thamesmead, or in *new towns, like Stevenage. ▷▷ urban renewal.

slump A form of *mass movement where rock and soil move downwards along a concave face.

slurry Liquid manure.

smog A combination of smoke and fog. The fog occurs naturally; the 'smoke' is introduced into the atmosphere by the activities of man. After the five-day-long period of smog in London in 1952, **smoke abatement** laws were introduced in Britain. ▷ photochemical smog.

snout The lower end, or terminus, of a valley *glacier.

snow Vapour from the atmosphere frozen into minute crystals which combine together to fall to the earth as light, white flakes.

social To do with society. The term **socio-economic status** refers to people's position in society, in terms of class, living standards, life-style, and income. Most *models of *urban structure identify distinct socio-economic areas.

softwood Easily worked wood obtained largely from fast-growing coniferous trees such as pine, spruce, and fir.

soil The upper layer of the ground, consisting of weathered rock, which supplies mineral particles, together with humus.

soil creep The slow, downslope movement of soil. Evidence for soil creep includes curved trees, leaning walls and telegraph poles. ▷▷ mass movement.

soil erosion The removal of the soil by wind and water,
and by the movement of soil downslope. The man-made
causes of soil erosion include the removal of windbreaks
and the exposure of bare earth, either by *overcropping or
by *overgrazing. Fire and strip-mining also accelerate the
erosion of the soil. ▷gullies.

soil profile A vertical series of soil *horizons down from
the ground surface to the parent rock.

soil texture The make-up of the soil, according to the
proportions of sand, silt, and clay present. ▷clay, sand,
silt.   ✍

Soil texture

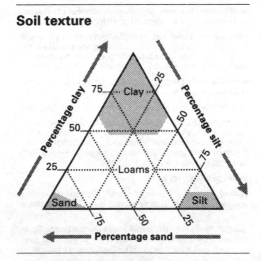

---

solar energy, solar power Any energy source based directly on the sun's radiation. Solar heat is trapped by an absorbent material, usually a black metal panel. The heat is then transferred to pipes which carry warmed air or water. In another method, the sun's rays may be centred on to one spot where the concentrated rays heat up a liquid in order to power a generator. The sun's radiation may be used also in solar cells which convert it into electricity. The chief advantage of solar energy is that, to all intents and purposes, it is inexhaustible. Its disadvantages include the fact that when it is most used for heating purposes, the days are short, the intensity of the rays is low, and the sun is often obscured by cloud.

solifluction The slow, downslope movement of saturated soil and rock fragments in areas with cold climates.

solstice The times, twice a year, when the poles lean furthest from the sun. In Britain, the **summer solstice** is the longest day—around 21 June; and the **winter solstice** is the shortest day—around 21 December.

solution The dissolving of a substance in water. Solution is an important form of *river erosion.

source The origin of a stream or river. ▷▷ river features.

South, the An alternative name for the *less developed world; that is, the less developed and least developed countries. The term was introduced in the *Brandt Report* (1980) to avoid any suggestion that 'more developed' indicated superiority over 'less developed'.

sown pasture *ley grass.

sparse Meagre, slight, light. Sparse *population density is less than 10 per km², sparse rainfall is less than 400 mm a year.

spatial Spread or distributed across the landscape. **Spatial analysis** is an important part of geography, and geographers look for patterns in the distribution of many features, ranging from *per capita GNP to annual *rainfall—in other words they look at **spatial distributions**.

Spearman's rank-correlation test This is a test to establish whether there is a *correlation between two sets of *variables such as daily calorie consumption and life expectancy. To run this test:

(i) In the first column, put the first set of variables in *rank order, starting with the highest statistic as number 1. List the ranks by the side of the numbers. If you have more than one reading of the same value, pencil in ranks for the 'places' they would occupy, thus:

Statistic	Rank
25	1
20	2
10	3
10	4
10	5
8	6

and then find the central value (*median) of the ranks you have pencilled in. Give these identical numbers that median rank (in this case it is 4):

Statistic	Rank
25	1
20	2
10	4
10	4
10	4

(ii) Put the relevant other half of the pairs of variables in the third column. Rank them as above, again writing in the numbers.

(iii) Subtract rank 2 from rank 1, putting the difference in ranks, d, in the fifth column.

(iv) Square all the values of d and put them into the d column.

(v) Add all the d values to find d.

(vi) Calculate the value of r_s, the *correlation coefficient*, using the equation:

$$r_s = \frac{1 - 6\Sigma d^2}{(n^3 - n)}$$

Where n is the number of pairs of variables.

For the meaning of the value of r_s, see *correlation coefficient.

sphere of influence Another name for the *urban field of a city.

spit A ridge of sand running away from the coast, usually with a curved seaward end. Spits grow in the prevailing direction of *longshore drift. Their ends are curved by the action of waves coming from different directions.
▷▷ marine deposition.

spoil heap, spoil tip A heap of waste left over from mining operations.

spring The point at which water emerges at the surface. A spring often marks the top of the *water-table, or occurs where a layer of *permeable rock lies above an *impermeable rock layer.

A **spring-line village** is one of a series of villages at the foot of a scarp through which water percolates until it emerges as a spring at the scarp foot. ✍

spring tide A *tide when the difference between high and low water is at its greatest. Spring tides happen twice a month, when the combined gravitational pull of the sun and moon is at its greatest.

Spring

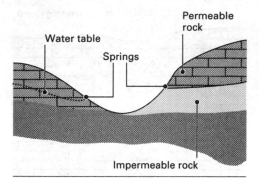

Water table

Permeable rock

Springs

Impermeable rock

spur A ridge of land, tapering at one end. ▷interlocking spur, truncated spur.

squatter settlement See shanty town.

SSSI *Site of Special Scientific Interest.

stack An isolated islet or pillar of rock standing up from the sea bed, close to the shore. A stack is the final feature formed when marine erosion attacks a cliff. ▷▷marine features.

stalactite A column of pure limestone hanging from the roof of a cave. It grows as an underground stream, deposits its dissolved load of calcium carbonate, and it may extend far enough to meet a *stalagmite and thus form a continuous column. ▷▷stalagmite.

stalagmite A column of pure limestone formed on the floor of a cave when the dissolved calcium carbonate in

Stalagmite

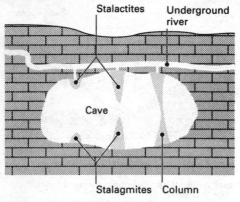

the underground water is deposited when the water evaporates as it splashes on to the cave floor.

standard of living Living standards are measured in many ways: among them are income, housing, education, leisure time, health, and life expectancy. ▷ Human Development Index, physical quality of life.

staple food The food—usually a carbohydrate—which provides the bulk of a person's energy. Rice, for example, is a staple in Asia; maize, yams, and cassava are staples in Africa, and potatoes are a staple in Europe.

statistic Any recorded measurement. **Statistics**, properly called **statistical methods** are the mathematical use of these measurements; common methods include the calculation of averages, the construction of *histograms, and *Spearman's rank-correlation test.

steel An alloy of iron which is less likely to fracture or rust.

step migration A form of *migration which takes place in stages; a young couple may move from the city to the inner suburbs when they have children and to the outer suburbs when they need more room for their growing children . . . and so on.

steppe The area of natural grassland stretching from central Europe to Siberia.

Stevenson screen A white, wooden box with louvred sides, standing on legs about 1 m above the ground, and made to house *meteorological instruments like rain gauges and maximum–minimum thermometers. The screen is designed to protect the instruments from strong winds and direct sun.

stolport A short take-off and short landing air*port*. Stolports are found in urban areas, where space is at a premium.

stone line One of a series of rough lines of stones, brought to the surface and sorted by the action of *frost in *periglacial regions. Although Britain no longer experiences periglacial conditions, some stone lines remain from the last *ice age.

storm beach Shingle thrown up above the normal high-water mark by very strong storm waves.

storm hydrograph A *hydrograph charting the effect of a rainstorm on the flow of a river.

storm surge An unusually high tide, caused by a combination of low pressure, on-shore winds, and high *spring tides.

stratum, plural **strata** In geology, a layer of distinctive deposits with surfaces roughly parallel to those above and below.

stream order The numbering of streams in a network. The most common method classes all unbranched streams as **first-order streams**. When two first-order streams meet, the resulting channel is a **second-order stream**. Where two second-order streams meet a **third-order stream** results, and so on.

striation A long scratch biting into a rock surface. Most **glacial striations** are a result of *abrasion by the frag-

Stream order

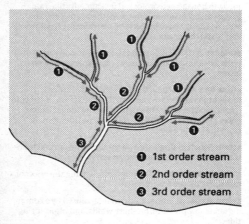

❶ 1st order stream
❷ 2nd order stream
❸ 3rd order stream

ments incorporated in the ice. These striations are only a few millimetres across.

subsidy A grant of money to make some form of economic activity possible—like a subsidy for growing oilseed rape, or to keep shop prices low. ▷hill-farming.

subsistence farming A form of agriculture where almost all the produce goes to feed and support the household and is not for sale. ▷peasant.

subsoil The soil below the layer normally used in cultivation, or below the depth to which most plant roots grow. It can be revealed by severe *soil erosion, or brought up by the type of very deep ploughing called **subsoiling**.

subtropical Referring to those areas lying between the Tropic of Cancer and 40° North, and the Tropic of Capricorn and 40° South.

suburbs, suburbia One-class communities located at the edge of the city and developed at low densities of housing per acre. **Suburbanization** is the creation of residential areas and, to some extent industry, at the edge of the city. It is the result of public transport, mass car ownership, pressure on space within the city, natural increase in the city which creates an increased demand for housing, and the growth of *footloose industries.

sulphur dioxide A chemical given off when most forms of coal are burned, and which combines with rain-water to form *acid rain.

sunshine recorder An instrument used to record the hours of sunshine in any day. An early form used a lens to concentrate the rays of the sun enough to burn a strip on a paper trace.

surface flow *overland flow.

suspended Hanging. Rivers carry much of their *load in **suspension**.

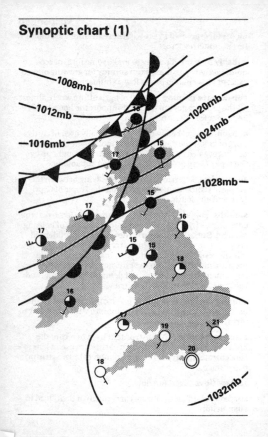

Synoptic chart (1)

Synoptic chart (2)

Fronts

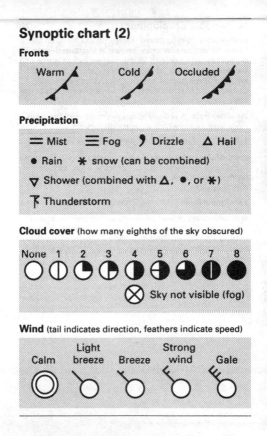

Warm   Cold   Occluded

Precipitation

= Mist   ≡ Fog   ❱ Drizzle   △ Hail

● Rain   ✳ snow (can be combined)

▽ Shower (combined with △, ●, or ✳)

⊤ Thunderstorm

Cloud cover (how many eighths of the sky obscured)

None 1 2 3 4 5 6 7 8

⊗ Sky not visible (fog)

Wind (tail indicates direction, feathers indicate speed)

Calm   Light breeze   Breeze   Strong wind   Gale

sustainable development Development based on the use of renewable resources, known as **sustained-yield resources** together with *conservation, lack of waste, and the attempt to limit *environmental damage. Much of Western development has squandered resources, and damaged the environment, and the earth cannot take the same process in the *less developed world.

swallow hole A vertical or near-vertical shaft in a limestone area, down which a stream disappears.

swash The water moving up a beach from a wave.

symbol An emblem or sign for something else. The meaning of the symbols on *maps is given in a key, and some symbols vary in size to indicate the importance of the feature they show.

syncline A downfold of rock *strata. ▷▷*fold.

synoptic chart A map on which are plotted the data of weather phenomena for a given area at a particular point in time. Pressure in *isobars is shown together with cloud cover, temperature, wind speed and direction, and *precipitation. ✍

synthetic fibre *artificial fibre.

T

taiga The coniferous forest found south of the *tundra in the northern continents.

take-off According to Rostow's theory of economic growth, this is the point at which a *pre-industrial society moves towards being an *industrial society. Take-off cannot occur without an adequate *infrastructure and more complex *technology.

tank irrigation In the Indian subcontinent, a type of *irrigation using a **tank**, in this case, a small lake or pool made by damming a stream to store the water brought by the *monsoon.

tariff A list of customs duties payable on *imports.

tarn A small mountain lake.

tax holiday The lifting, by a government, of taxes on a business for a number of years. Tax holidays are granted in an effort to attract new industries from abroad, but many firms move their businesses to another country when the 'holiday' period is over.

technology Tools, machinery, and techniques. ▷ appropriate technology, high technology, intermediate technology.

tectonic To do with the large-scale processes acting to shape the earth's *crust, especially the movement of *plates.

temperate Moderate. A **temperate climate** has few *extremes of temperature: average summer temperatures

are around 20 °C, average winter temperatures around
0 °C, and annual rainfall is around 800 mm.

temperature A measurement of heat. Any **temperature
range**, whether *annual or *diurnal, is calculated by sub-
tracting the lowest from the highest temperature. **Temperature change** in a climate is usually a part of a
*climatic change. ▷greenhouse effect, isotherm, heat
island.

tenure ▷housing tenure, land tenure .

terminal moraine See moraine.

terms of trade The relationship within a country
between the prices of imports and exports. The trend in
this century has been for cheap primary products and
expensive manufactured goods. This has affected *less
developed countries very badly, because they tend to
export raw materials and import finished goods. As a
result, many Third World countries have adopted policies
of *industrialization, and *import substitution.

terrace 1. See river terrace. 2. One of a series of flat
'steps' in a sloping field, built to make more land available
for cultivation, and to cut down *soil erosion. The cutting
of terraces is known as **terracing**.

tertiary industry Any industry concerned with the provision of *services, such as health, education, or *retailing.
That part of a country's economy which is involved with
tertiary industry is known as the **tertiary sector**.

thematic map A map drawn to illustrate a particular feature, such as *climate, or *global variations in per capita
*GNP.

theme park The first theme park was Disneyland, California, opened in 1955. The idea has been taken up in Britain
and elsewhere. Theme parks developed as a response to
increased leisure and increased spending power.

thermal To do with heat. A **thermal power-station** makes electricity by boiling water to make the steam which turns the generators. ▷conventional power-station, nuclear power.

thermometer An instrument used to measure *temperature.

Third World A term used for the *less developed countries. It was devised to distinguish these countries from the capitalist *First World and the communist Second World. Some people have objected to the term, arguing that 'Third' means 'third in importance', but this is not implied.

threshold population The number of people in a *central place, or within its catchment area, necessary to justify the provision of a *good or *service. For example, in Britain, a primary school will be set up when the threshold population is around 4000; a cinema when the threshold population is around 60 000. Threshold populations vary between different nations; the threshold population for a baker's shop is about 2000 in Britain but about 600 in France.

throughflow The movement of water through the soil. ▷hydrological cycle.

thunder When a stroke of lightning passes through the atmosphere, the air becomes intensely hot, perhaps to 30 000 *C. The heat causes the air to expand violently, and this causes a shock wave which is heard as thunder. A **thunderstorm** is a period of heavy rain with thunder and lightning.

tidal To do with the *tide. The **tidal range** is the difference between the lowest and highest tides, and the **tidal limit** is either the lowest or highest normal tide. For **tidal wave**, see tsunami.

tidal energy Energy based on the motions of the *tide. Schemes to use tidal energy have been implemented at the Rance Barrage Tidal Scheme near St Malo, and on the east coast of Canada. Both of these sites have a large *tidal range.

tide The twice daily rise and fall of sea-level. Tides are the result of the pull exerted on the earth by the gravity of the moon and of the sun. This pull affects the land masses as well as the oceans but the reaction of the water is much greater and much more apparent. All of the earth is attracted by the moon's gravity but the greatest effect is exerted on each side of the earth as it faces the moon. The moon 'pulls out' two bulges of water from these sides. These bulges are fixed and the earth moves through them. This gives high water twice daily.

Tide

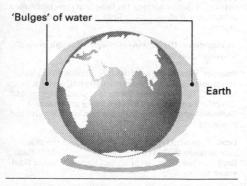

Moon

'Bulges' of water

Earth

The sun also attracts water. When the effects of both sun and moon coincide, twice monthly, in the second and fourth quarters of the moon, high *spring tides occur. When the forces of the moon and sun are opposed to each other, lower, *neap tides are the result.   ✍

till Till is the substance which *moraines are made of. It is the sediment which is deposited directly below a glacier, and till particles range in size from fine clay to rock fragments and boulders.

TNC See transnational corporation.

tombolo A *spit which joins an offshore island to the mainland. ▷▷ marine deposition.

topography *relief.

topological map A map designed to show only a selected feature, such as the stations on the London Underground. Locations are shown as dots, with straight lines connecting them. Actual shapes and scale are not important. A **topological transformation** is a map based on something other than linear distances, such as the one below which shows New Zealand in terms of travelling time.   ✍

topsoil The cultivated soil; the surface soil as opposed to the *subsoil.

tor A detached mass of *jointed and *weathered granite, found on a moor.

tourism Making a holiday involving an overnight stay away from someone's usual home. (Compare with *recreation.) Urban tourist centres tend to have an unusually high number of shops and services, while tourism in the *less developed countries can provide the income for economic development. Not everyone is in favour of tourism in the less developed countries. It is argued that tourism spoils the *environment, does not benefit local people, and causes local people to become dissatisfied when they see much higher living standards than they are used to.

trade The movements of goods from producers to consumers. Trading takes place between two groups when each can make a commodity at the same standard more cheaply than the other can. Countries which import much more than they export have a **trade gap** which is reflected in a negative *balance of payments. In such cases, many governments try to protect their own industries by imposing *tariffs and customs duties, but this can lead to a **trade war** as country after country raises barriers to trade. ▷GATT.

Topological transformation

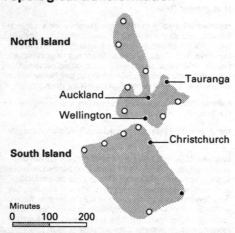

North Island

Tauranga

Auckland

Wellington

Christchurch

South Island

Minutes
0   100   200

trade winds The tropical easterlies, blowing from the *subtropical anticyclones towards the equator, at a fairly constant speed. ▷▷ general circulation of the atmosphere.

trading bloc A group of countries which has tried to increase trade within the group by abolishing many *tariffs and lowering customs duties. Examples include the European Union (EU) and the Association of South-East Asian Nations (ASEAN).

trading estate *industrial estate.

trading nation Whilst all states sell their exports and buy in imports, there are wide differences in the volume of trade handled. The greater part of world trade flows between the *more developed countries, and the great trading nations today, like Japan, have a favourable *balance of trade, an *advanced economy, and a reliable currency. ▷ GATT, international division of labour.

traffic artery A major road.

traffic calming Slowing down the speed of the traffic, especially in *residential areas. The methods in common use are speed ramps (sleeping policemen), increasing the numbers of pedestrian crossings, and building a series of low walls, half-way across the road, but on alternate sides.

transcurrent fault A *fault where the movement has been more or less horizontal, and across the slope of the fault plane. ▷▷ fault.

transhumance A seasonal movement of men and animals between different grazing grounds. Shepherds leave their lowland, winter quarters, and move to upland, summer pastures. Transhumance used to be common practice in the Alps, but is now relatively rare.

transition zone *zone in transition.

transmigration The relocation of large numbers of people as a result of a government plan. The most important example is the movement within Indonesia of people from Java to Irian Jaya.

transnational corporation (TNC) A very large company, like Ford or Nestlé, with offices, factories, and branches in many countries. Third World governments try to attract TNCs by granting *tax holidays or ready-made factories, but many TNCs move elsewhere when the 'holiday' period comes to an end. It is not unusual for a TNC to send the components of a good, like a calculator, to a *less developed country to have it assembled where labour costs are low. ▷ international division of labour.

transpiration The release of water through the leaves of plants.

tree line, timber line The line above which trees will not grow. This occurs at high latitudes, for example when the conifers of the *taiga gives way to *tundra, or at high altitudes.

tributary A river which flows into another, usually larger one. ▷▷ river features.

trickle irrigation Irrigating by using a hose with a number of small holes, each hole beside a plant. In this way, there is less water loss than by soaking the whole of the field. Trickle irrigation is an example of *intermediate technology.

tropic One of two lines of *latitude, 23° 30' away from the equator; the Tropic of Capricorn lying to the south of the equator and the Tropic of Cancer to the north. These two mark the boundaries of that part of the earth which experiences overhead sun. The term **tropical** refers to the parts of the earth which lie between the Tropics of Cancer and Capricorn.

tropical cyclone, tropical revolving storm Alternative terms for *hurricane.

tropical rain forest A *tropical forest of trees which typically have * buttress roots, long, straight lower trunks, and leathery leaves. The trees seem to grow in distinct layers: the upper layer, at around 30 m; the intermediate layer at 20–25 m; and the lower layer at around 10–15 m. There is little undergrowth because little light breaks through the canopy of trees, but lianas (creepers) are common. The trees flower, fruit, and shed their leaves at random; there is no clear pattern of seasons. The range of plant and animal species is immense and many plants yield important medicinal compounds. The felling of the rain forest causes soil erosion, the destruction of potentially useful species, and the smoke of burning logs increases the quantity of carbon dioxide in the atmosphere. Some experts believe that the *climates and *hydrology of the earth may be altered if the tropical rain forest is destroyed. ▷ greenhouse effect ▷▷ natural vegetation.

trough *glacial trough.

truncated Cut off. A **truncated spur** is a *spur where the lower, projecting end has been removed by *glacial erosion. ▷▷ glacial erosion.

tsunami A huge sea wave. Most are formed as a result of earthquakes. In 1992, a tsunami resulting from an earthquake engulfed the island of Timor, causing thousands of deaths.

tube well A *well created by drilling a borehole and lining it with piping.

tuff A rock made from hardened volcanic *ash.

tundra The barren plains of northern Canada, the USA, and Eurasia. Temperatures and rainfall are low, so that only hardy shrubs, mosses, and lichens can grow. The lower soil is permanently frozen, so that drainage is poor, and this makes marshes and swamps common in summer. ▷ permafrost.

twilight area, twilight zone The run-down area of a town, often the inner city, or the *zone in transition.

typhoon Another term for *hurricane.

U

underdeveloped The original meaning of this word was that existing resources had not been greatly used, but it now means that living standards are low. ▷least developed country, less developed country, Third World. It is true that some oil-rich underdeveloped countries, like Saudi Arabia, have high incomes, which are enjoyed by a few, but there are other indicators of **underdevelopment** besides per capita *GNP, and these include: high birth rates, high infant mortality, undernourishment, a large agricultural and small industrial sector, high levels of illiteracy, and low life expectancy. ▷development, development indicators, Human Development Index, physical quality of life.

underemployment A situation when *either* too many people are doing a job, *or* when large numbers are without work.

underground water *groundwater.

undernourishment Lack of sufficient food.

undertow The strong pull exerted by the *backwash of a receding wave.

unmetalled road A road not finished with tarmac, cement, or asphalt; it may be made of rough fragments of stone or simply consist of two muddy wheel-tracks. Many of the roads in *less developed countries are unmetalled; this makes them harder to use in wet weather.

upland *highland.

urban To do with a city or town. No standard population totals have been given for the point at which a settlement becomes a town or city; in Iceland, a settlement of 300 people is classed as urban but the figure is 10 000 in Spain.

urban decay, urban blight The running down of part of a city. Some parts of the city become overcrowded, and some become outdated as buildings age. Large houses, once family homes, become multi-occupied. Better-off people and businesses move out, and as neighbourhoods decline, vandalism increases. ▷ urban renewal, redlining, slum, twilight zone.

Urban Development Corporation (UDC) An organization set up by the UK central government to speed up *urban renewal in *depressed areas.

Urban field

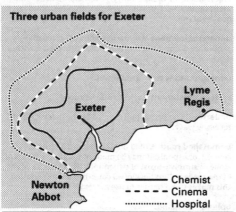

Three urban fields for Exeter

Lyme Regis

Exeter

Newton Abbot

——— Chemist
- - - - Cinema
·············· Hospital

urban field This is the area surrounding a city and which is influenced by it. It is difficult to find an exact boundary for an urban field; for example, the area served by a city newspaper may not be the same as the area served by the city's public transport. Here are two methods:

(i) Find out from the offices of any newspaper produced in the city the limit of where they deliver their paper for sale. Plot this boundary on a map.

(ii) If there is a city-based bus company, find out from the bus company offices the limit of *local* bus services. Plot this boundary on a map.   ✍

urban geography The study of the sites, growth, *morphology, and classification of towns.

urbanization The increase in the proportion of the population of a region, country, or the world, which lives in towns and cities. This occurs through *rural–urban migration and through *natural increase within *urban areas. ▷ pull factor, rural depopulation.

urban morphology The layout of a town, particularly in terms of its *land use. Most towns have definite zones : different classes and dates of housing, shopping and office areas, and industrial areas. Several geographers have tried to build *models of urban morphology. ▷ Burgess model, sector model, multiple nuclei model.   ✍

urban renewal The attempt to bring back prosperity to run-down urban areas. Sometimes whole areas are cleared and new housing, retail, or office developments put in place; examples include the redevelopment of London's Docklands. In other cases, existing houses are up-graded (*gentrification), or it may be that a derelict district is turned into an urban wildlife area in an effort to improve the *amenities of the surrounding neighbourhoods. ▷ urban decay.

urban sprawl The extension of the city into the country-side. Planners have tried to stop this growth by establish-

Urban morphology

- **A** Allotments
- **B** Fringe development
- **C** Cemetery
- **D** Commuter village
- **E** Sewage works
- **F** Park
- **G** Factory
- **H** Hospital
- ☐ Terraced housing
- ⦀ Semi detatched

ing *green belts around the city. ▷conurbation, ribbon development.

U-shaped valley Another term for a *glacial trough.

V

valley A long area of lowland, usually broader at its head than at its mouth, cut by a river.

variable A changing factor which may affect or be affected by another.

velocity Speed. The **velocity of flow** of a river is the distance travelled by the river water per second. Average velocity tends to increase as you go downstream.

village A small settlement, usually (in Britain) with a shop, a church, and a pub (but see dormitory village).

viscous Sticky or gluey. **Viscosity** is the ease with which a substance can flow.

volcano An opening of the *crust out of which *lava, *ash, and gases erupt. The shape and ferocity of a volcano when it erupts depend very much on the type of lava it produces. Steep-sided *cone volcanoes are associated with thick (*viscous) lava and much ash, and these often erupt violently; while more gently sloping volcanoes are formed when runnier lava wells up quite quietly, and spreads over a large area. Most volcanoes are located at *plate margins. ▷active volcano, natural hazard. ▷▷volcanic features.

volcanic features These include *calderas, *cones, *craters and *crater lakes, *lava, *magma, *pyroclasts, and *tuff.

Volcanic features

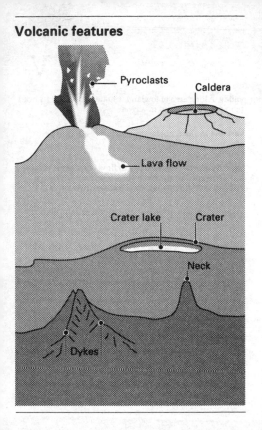

Von Thünen (1)

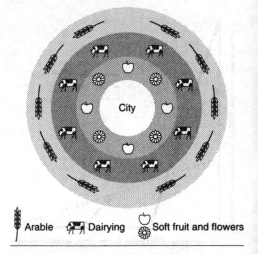

🌾 Arable   🐄 Dairying   🌼 Soft fruit and flowers

---

von Thünen theory A *model of *agricultural *land use patterns, based on transport costs, which vary with the bulkiness and perishability of the product:

• Products in group A, like soft fruits, and flowers, are perishable or costly to transport, but have a high market price and are therefore farmed near the city.
• Products in group B, like butter and cheese, sell for less but have lower transport costs. At a certain point, group B products become more profitable than group A, because of lower transport costs.

Von Thünen (2)

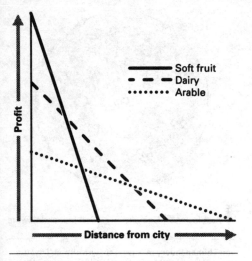

Soft fruit
Dairy
Arable

Profit

Distance from city

• Products in group C, like wheat, are of low value but are easy and cheap to transport. Eventually, group C products become the most profitable. The changing pattern of the most profitable product is therefore seen as a series of land use rings around the city.

This theory may also be shown as a graph, with the most profitable group at any point being the highest line on the graph.

V-shaped valley A term used to describe an unglaciated river valley because its *cross-section looks like a very open V.

vulcanicity *volcanic action.

W

wadi In *arid areas, a steep-sided valley, which is usually quite dry, but can contain a short-lived torrent after a rare rainstorm.

warehousing Storing goods after they have been produced by a factory, but before they are sent to the shops. ▷retail.

warm anticyclone An area of high pressure brought about when high-level air is forced downwards. It brings calm, clear, and warm weather. ▷anticyclone.

warm sector The central wedge of a *depression.

water cycle Another term for the *hydrological cycle.

waterfall A point on a river where water falls vertically. Waterfalls may be found at a band of more resistant rock, or at *knick points.

water gap A pass through an upland or ridge which has been cut by a river. A classic example is found at Corfe, in Dorset.

waterlogged Saturated with water. **Waterlogging** occurs after heavy rain, especially in *clay soils, or when the soil is underlain by *impermeable rocks. ▷▷ hydrological cycle.

watershed The boundary between two river systems, marking the divide between *drainage basins.

water supply Water is used both domestically—in people's homes—and by industries, and as a nation becomes more developed, the demand for water rises. In

Britain, in addition, demand is often highest where rainfall is lowest. Solutions to this problem include: recycling
water, building more *reservoirs, constructing water
pipelines, and pumping out more *groundwater. Each has
its difficulties, so Water Boards are now thinking of meter-
ing water so that people will use less. In *less developed
countries, the problem is not simply lack of water, but
lack of *clean* water; thousands, especially children, die of
water-borne diseases. The richer Third World countries
with a sea coast can purify their water by desalination, but
this is not an option for the poorer ones. A further problem, which can affect *more developed and *less developed
alike is when an upstream nation takes out so much water
from a river that not enough is left for the country downstream. The extraction of Nile water by Sudan may well
lead to shortages in Egypt.

water-table The level below which the ground is saturated; the upper surface of the *groundwater. Any hole in
the ground will fill with water when the water-table has
been reached. The level of the water-table often fluctuates,
falling in dry weather and rising in wet. ▷▷ hydrological
cycle.

water vapour Water when it is in the form of a gas.

wave A ridge of water between two lower sections. As
waves reach the shore, they curl into an arc and break, and
the energy of surface waves contributes to the *erosion of
the coast. **Wave power** is a possible *alternative source of
power which uses this energy, but it has yet to be developed commercially. Waves are also a vital factor in *longshore drift.

wave-built platform A flat area of sediments, just seaward of a wave-cut platform.

wave-cut platform A very gently sloping, level area of
solid rock, stretching seawards from the base of a cliff, and
also known as an *abrasion platform.

Wave refraction

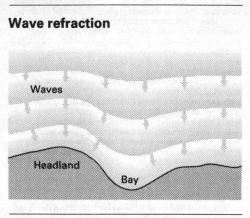

Waves

Headland

Bay

wave refraction The change in the approach angle of a wave as it moves towards the shore. As water shallows, waves slow down. This change in speed causes the straight line of a wave to 'bend'. Refraction causes waves to converge on *headlands and spread out in *bays. This means that the energy of the waves is concentrated on the headlands rather than on the beaches. ✍

weather The events occurring in the *atmosphere at any one place or time. This includes conditions of *atmospheric pressure, *humidity, *temperature, *sunshine hours, *cloud cover, wind speed and direction, visibility, and *precipitation (*fog, *rain, *snow, *sleet, and *frost). A **weather station** contains the equipment necessary to record these conditions:

Condition	Instrument used
*Atmospheric pressure	*Barometer
*Relative humidity	Whirling hygrometer
*Temperature	Maximum–minimum thermometer
Sunshine hours	*Sunshine recorder
Wind speed	*Anemometer
Wind direction	*Weather vane
Precipitation	*Rain gauge

The readings from many weather stations form the raw data which weather forecasters work from.

weathering The breakdown, but not the removal, of rocks. ▷biological weathering, chemical weathering, physical weathering.

West, the Another loose term for the capitalist economies of the world; the First World.

westerlies, Winds blowing *from* the west, most often occurring in the mid-latitudes, or temperate areas. The westerlies are important *prevailing winds in the *general circulation of the atmosphere.

wetland A naturally occurring area of saturated soils, such as *fens or marshes. Many wetlands are being drained in order to use them as farmland, and this is destroying the habitat of a number of species.

whirling hygrometer An instrument used to measure *relative humidity. It consists of two *thermometers, one of which is dry and the other of which is kept wet by dampening the material which covers it. The hygrometer is whirled around in the air, and the readings of both thermometers are taken. A statistical table is used to convert these two readings into a measurement of the relative humidity.

white-collar worker A term for non-manual workers.

willy-willy The Australian term for a *hurricane.

wind belt A zone of the earth, where certain *prevailing winds, such as the *westerlies or the trade winds, predominate. ▷▷general circulation of the atmosphere.

wind deposition As wind speeds fall, any material carried by the wind will be deposited. *Sand-dunes are the most important features of wind deposition. ▷▷desert features.

wind energy Power generated by harnessing the wind, usually by windmills. Early windmills were used to power millstones, pumps, and forges. Electricity can be, and is, generated by the wind; but there are drawbacks: the wind does not blow constantly, a large site is necessary, and some people object to the appearance, and noise, of modern windmills.

wind erosion The removal of material by the force of the wind. Loose material is easily blown away, but resistant material is 'sand-blasted' by the *abrasive power of particles carried along by the wind. Features of wind erosion include *yardangs and *zeugen. ▷▷desert features.

wind gap A pass through an upland or ridge which is not occupied by a river. It may be that the gap was cut by a river which has now been diverted, or has simply dried up.

wind vane A pivoting needle which will line up with the wind and thus show wind direction.

wold A local term for an upland, such as the Cotswolds, or the Yorkshire Wolds.

woodland Woodlands may be *deciduous, *coniferous, or mixed, and they may be natural, or deliberately planted. ▷forestry.

Y

yardang In a desert area, a long ridge which has been isolated as the wind has removed the rocks on either side. Yardangs can be 100 m or more in height and can stretch for many kilometres. ▷▷ wind erosion.

yield The product, or end result, of any activity. Crop yields are usually reckoned in yield per *unit area*, such as a hectare, or an acre, but output can also be expressed in yield per *person*. In *intensive agriculture, both types of yield are high; in *extensive agriculture, yields per unit area are low.

Z

zero population growth (ZPG) The point at which the population of the world remains stationary. This could be brought about by contraception, but will probably not occur until poor people no longer need to depend on their children. ▷ demographic transition model.

zeuge, plural **zeugen** An upstanding rock capped with a harder layer and undercut at the base by *wind erosion.

zone of discard, zone in transition That area of a city which was once a part of the *CBD, but is now in decline, and is characterized by low status shops and warehouses, and vacant or derelict property. ▷ Burgess model.

ZPG *zero population growth.

Datafile

The countries in the datafile are listed in order of their
rating in the Human Development Index (see dictionary).
Most of the statistics come from the UNDP *Human
Development Report, 1993* (OUP); those marked with an
asterisk come from *The State of the World's Children*, 1987
(also OUP). The indicators are measured as follows:

Birth rate = births per 1000 people, per year.
Death rate = deaths per 1000 people, per year.
Infant mortality rate = deaths per 1000 children under 12
months old.
Life expectancy is in years.
Per capita *GNP is expressed in $US.
Commercial energy consumption per capita is expressed
in kg oil equivalent.

Japan

Human Development Index rating 1
Birth rate 13
Death rate 7
Infant mortality rate 6
Life expectancy 78.6
Per capita *GNP $US25 840
Workers in agriculture 7%
Adult literacy rate 99.0%
Population urbanized 76%
Commercial energy consumption per capita 3563

USA

Human Development Index rating 6
Birth rate 16
Death rate 9
Infant mortality rate 11
Life expectancy 75.9
Per capita *GNP $US21 810
Workers in agriculture 3%
Adult literacy rate 99.0%
Population urbanized 74%
Commercial energy consumption per capita 7822

Australia

Human Development Index rating 7
Birth rate 16
Death rate 8
Infant mortality rate 9
Life expectancy 76.5
Per capita *GNP $US16 560
Workers in agriculture 15%
Adult literacy rate 99.0%
Population urbanized 86%
Commercial energy consumption per capita 5041

France
Human Development Index rating 8
Birth rate 14
Death rate 11
Infant mortality rate 8
Life expectancy 76.4
Per capita *GNP $US19590
Workers in agriculture 7%
Adult literacy rate 99.0%
Population urbanized 73%
Commercial energy consumption per capita 3845

Netherlands
Human Development Index rating 9
Birth rate 12
Death rate 9
Infant mortality rate 8
Life expectancy 77.2
Per capita *GNP $US17570
Workers in agriculture 5%
Adult literacy rate 99.0%
Population urbanized 88%
Commercial energy consumption per capita 5123

United Kingdom
Human Development Index rating 10
Birth rate 13
Death rate 12
Infant mortality rate 10
Life expectancy 75.7
Per capita *GNP $US16080
Workers in agriculture 2%
Adult literacy rate 99.0%
Population urbanized 92%
Commercial energy consumption per capita 3646

Germany

Human Development Index rating 12
Birth rate 12
Death rate 12
Infant mortality rate 10
Life expectancy 75.2
Per capita *GNP $US22 360
Workers in agriculture 4%
Adult literacy rate 99.0%
Population urbanized 81%
Commercial energy consumption per capita 3491

Denmark

Human Development Index rating 13
Birth rate 11
Death rate 11
Infant mortality rate 8
Life expectancy 75.8
Per capita *GNP $US22 440
Workers in agriculture 4%
Adult literacy rate 99.0%
Population urbanized 86%
Commercial energy consumption per capita 3618

Belgium

Human Development Index rating 16
Birth rate 12
Death rate 12
Infant mortality rate 9
Life expectancy 75.2
Per capita *GNP $US17 580
Workers in agriculture 3%
Adult literacy rate 99.0%
Population urbanized 96%
Commercial energy consumption per capita 2807

Republic of Ireland
Human Development Index rating 21
Birth rate 21
Death rate 9
Infant mortality rate 10
Life expectancy 74.6
Per capita *GNP $US10370
Workers in agriculture 13%
Adult literacy rate 99.0%
Population urbanized 57%
Commercial energy consumption per capita 2653

Italy
Human Development Index rating 22
Birth rate 14
Death rate 13
Infant mortality rate 11
Life expectancy 76.0
Per capita *GNP $US16880
Workers in agriculture 9%
Adult literacy rate 97.1%
Population urbanized 67%
Commercial energy consumption per capita 2764

Spain
Human Development Index rating 23
Birth rate 15
Death rate 9
Infant mortality rate 10
Life expectancy 77.0
Per capita *GNP $US11010
Workers in agriculture 10%
Adult literacy rate 97.5%
Population urbanized 76%
Commercial energy consumption per capita 2201

Datafile

Greece

Human Development Index rating 25
Birth rate 15
Death rate 10
Infant mortality rate 14
Life expectancy 76.1
Per capita *GNP $US6010
Workers in agriculture 22%
Adult literacy rate 93.2%
Population urbanized 60%
Commercial energy consumption per capita 2092

Russian Federation

Human Development Index rating 37
Birth rate 19
Death rate 9
Infant mortality rate 24
Life expectancy 69.3
Per capita *GNP *not available*
Workers in agriculture (estimated) 12%
Adult literacy rate 94.0%
Population urbanized 66%
Commercial energy consumption per capita *not available*

Portugal

Human Development Index rating 41
Birth rate 17
Death rate 10
Infant mortality rate 19
Life expectancy 74.0
Per capita *GNP $US4950
Workers in agriculture 17%
Adult literacy rate 85.0%
Population urbanized 31%
Commercial energy consumption per capita 1507

Mexico
Human Development Index rating 53
Birth rate 33
Death rate 7
Infant mortality rate 37
Life expectancy 69.7
Per capita *GNP $US2490
Workers in agriculture 22%
Adult literacy rate 87.6%
Population urbanized 70%
Commercial energy consumption per capita 1300

Malaysia
Human Development Index rating 57
Birth rate 29
Death rate 6
Infant mortality rate 15
Life expectancy 69.7
Per capita *GNP $US2330
Workers in agriculture 13%
Adult literacy rate 78.4%
Population urbanized 38%
Commercial energy consumption per capita 974

Brazil
Human Development Index rating 70
Birth rate 30
Death rate 8
Infant mortality rate 59
Life expectancy 65.6
Per capita *GNP $US2680
Workers in agriculture 28%
Adult literacy rate 81.1%
Population urbanized 73%
Commercial energy consumption per capita 915

Saudi Arabia

Human Development Index rating 84
Birth rate 41
Death rate 8
Infant mortality rate 78
Life expectancy 64.5
Per capita *GNP $US7070
Workers in agriculture 48%
Adult literacy rate 70.0%
Population urbanized 72%
Commercial energy consumption per capita 5033

Egypt

Human Development Index rating 124
Birth rate 35
Death rate 11
Infant mortality rate 93
Life expectancy 64.5
Per capita *GNP $US640
Workers in agriculture 34%
Adult literacy rate 48.4%
Population urbanized 46%
Commercial energy consumption per capita 598

Papua New Guinea

Human Development Index rating 129
Birth rate 37
Death rate 13
Infant mortality rate 68
Life expectancy 54.9
Per capita *GNP $US850
Workers in agriculture 76%
Adult literacy rate 52.0%
Population urbanized 14%
Commercial energy consumption per capita 233

India
Human Development Index rating 134
Birth rate 30
Death rate 12
Infant mortality rate 90
Life expectancy 54.9
Per capita *GNP $US850
Workers in agriculture 62%
Adult literacy rate 48.2%
Population urbanized 26%
Commercial energy consumption per capita 231

Nigeria
Human Development Index rating 142
Birth rate 50
Death rate 16
Infant mortality rate 99
Life expectancy 54.9
Per capita *GNP $US850
Workers in agriculture 43%
Adult literacy rate 50.7%
Population urbanized 23%
Commercial energy consumption per capita 138